The Unofficial Guide to
Walt Disney World®
& EPCOT® —

Also available from Prentice Hall Trade Division:

The Unofficial Guide to Disneyland, by Bob Sehlinger

The Unofficial Guide to
Walt Disney World®
& EPCOT®

New and Revised
Third Edition

Bob Sehlinger
John Finley

PRENTICE HALL
NEW YORK

Produced by Menasha Ridge Press

Published by Prentice Hall Trade Division
A division of Simon & Schuster, Inc.
Gulf + Western Building
One Gulf + Western Plaza
New York, New York 10023

Manufactured in the United States of America

Library of Congress Cataloging-in-Publication Data
Sehlinger, Bob, 1945–
    The unofficial guide to Walt Disney World & EPCOT.
    "Produced by Menasha Ridge Press"–T.p. verso.
    Includes index.
    I. Walt Disney World (Fla.)—Guide-books.   2. EPCOT
(Fla.)—Guide-books.   I. Finley, John, 1938–
II. Title.
GV1853.3.F62W3468   1989   791'.06'875924   88-25461
ISBN: 0–13–942905–0

10 9 8 7 6 5 4 3 2 I

ISBN: 0–13–942905–0

Declaration of Independence

The authors and researchers of this guide specifically and categorically declare that they are and always have been totally independent of Walt Disney Productions, Inc., of Disneyland, Inc., of Walt Disney World, Inc., and of any and all other members of the Disney corporate family not listed.

The material in this guide originated with the authors and researchers and has not been reviewed, edited, or in any way approved by Walt Disney Productions, Inc., Disneyland, Inc., or Walt Disney World, Inc.

Trademarks

The following attractions, shows, components, entities, etc., mentioned or discussed in this guide are registered trademarks of Walt Disney Productions, Inc.:

Adventureland
AudioAnimatronics
Captain EO
Disneyland
EPCOT
Fantasyland
Magic Kingdom
New Orleans Square
PeopleMover
Space Mountain
Walt Disney
Walt Disney World

New trademarks are applied for almost continuously. These will be recognized as and when appropriate in subsequent editions of this guide.

Contents

Acknowledgments   xiii

How Come "Unofficial"?   3

How This Guide Was Researched and Written   4

Walt Disney World—An Overview   6
> What Walt Disney World Encompasses – 6   The Major Theme
> Parks – 7   The Swimming Theme Parks – 8   The Minor Theme
> Parks – 12   Should I Go to Walt Disney World If I've Been to
> Disneyland in California? – 13

PART ONE—*Planning Before You Leave Home*

Gathering Information   19

Timing Your Visit   20
> Trying to Reason with the Tourist Season – 20   Florida Traffic
> Patterns – 22   When to Go to Walt Disney World – 24   Operating
> Hours – 26   Official Opening Time vs. Real Opening Time – 26
> Packed Park Compensation Plan – 27

A Word About Lodging   29
> Staying in the World – 29   Lodging Outside of Walt Disney
> World – 32

Getting There   34
> Directions – 34   The Parking Situation – 34   Taking a Tram or
> Shuttle Bus from Your Hotel – 36   Disney-MGM Studios and
> Typhoon Lagoon Parking – 36

Making the Most of Your Time   37
> Allocating Time – 37   Prices Subject to Change Without
> Notice – 37   Admission Options – 38   Which Park to See
> First – 39   Optimum Touring Situation – 39   Seeing Walt Disney
> World on a Tight Schedule – 42   One-Day Touring – 42   Touring
> Plans: What They Are and How They Work – 44   Letters,
> Comments, and Questions from Readers – 47   Walt Disney World
> Vacations Guided by the Authors – 47

PART TWO—*Tips and Warnings*

Credit Cards – 51   Rain – 51   Small Children – 51   Visitors with Special Needs – 54
• Handicapped Visitors   • Foreign Language Assistance
• Messages   • Car Trouble   • Lost and Found
Excuse Me, but Where Can I Find . . . – 55
• Someplace to Put All These Packages?   • A Mixed Drink or a Beer?   • Some Rain Gear?   • A Cure for This Headache?   • A Prescription Filled?   • Suntan Lotion?   • A Smoke?
• Feminine Hygiene Products?   • Cash?   • A Place to Exchange Foreign Currency?   • A Place to Leave My Pet?
• Film?

PART THREE—*The Magic Kingdom*

Arriving and Getting Oriented – 61   Starting the Tour – 61

Main Street, U.S.A.   63

Main Street Services – 63   Main Street Attractions – 64   Walt Disney World Railroad – 64   *Walt Disney Story* – 65   Main Street Cinema – 65   Main Street Minor Attractions – 66   Main Street Restaurants and Shops – 66

Adventureland   68

Swiss Family Treehouse – 68   Jungle Cruise – 69   Pirates of the Caribbean – 69   *Tropical Serenade (Enchanted Tiki Birds)* – 70   Adventureland Eateries and Shops – 70

Frontierland   71

Big Thunder Mountain Railroad – 71   *Diamond Horseshoe Jamboree* – 72   *Country Bear Jamboree* – 73   Tom Sawyer Island – 73   Davy Crockett's Explorer Canoes – 74   Frontierland Shootin' Gallery – 75   Walt Disney World Railroad – 75   Frontierland Eateries and Shops – 76

Liberty Square   77

Hall of Presidents – 77   Liberty Square Riverboat – 78   Haunted Mansion – 78   Mike Fink Keelboats – 79   Liberty Square Eateries and Shops – 80

Fantasyland   81

It's a Small World – 81   Skyway to Tomorrowland – 82   Peter Pan's Flight – 83   *Magic Journeys* – 83   Cinderella's Golden Carrousel – 84   Mr. Toad's Wild Ride – 84   Snow White's Scary

Adventures – 85   20,000 Leagues Under the Sea – 85   Dumbo, the Flying Elephant – 86   Mad Tea Party – 87   Fantasyland Eateries and Shops – 88

Mickey's Birthdayland   89
Mickey's Surprise Party – 90   Other Mickey's Birthdayland Attractions – 91   Grandma Duck's Petting Farm – 91   Small Children's Play Area – 92

Tomorrowland   93
Space Mountain – 93   Grand Prix Raceway – 95   Skyway to Fantasyland – 96   StarJets – 96   WEDway PeopleMover – 97   *Carousel of Progress* – 98   Dreamflight – 98   World Premier Circle-Vision: *American Journeys* – 99   *Mission to Mars* – 100   Tomorrowland Eateries and Shops – 100

Magic Kingdom Ride Information   101
Cutting Down Your Time in Line by Understanding the Rides – 101
Magic Kingdom Theater Information   105
Cutting Down Your Time in Line by Understanding the Shows – 105
How to Deal with Obnoxious People – 106
Live Entertainment in the Magic Kingdom   107
Eating in the Magic Kingdom   110
Shopping in the Magic Kingdom   113

Magic Kingdom One-Day Touring Plans   114
Traffic Patterns in the Magic Kingdom   115
Magic Kingdom One-Day Touring Plan, for Adults   117
Outline of Magic Kingdom One-Day Touring Plan, for Adults   123
Outline of Magic Kingdom One-Day Touring Plan, for Parents with Small Children   127
Not to be Missed at the Magic Kingdom   130
Table Summary   131

PART FOUR—EPCOT Center
Contrasting EPCOT Center and the Magic Kingdom – 135
Arriving and Getting Oriented – 136

Future World   139
Spaceship Earth – 139   Earth Station – 140   CommuniCore – 140   Attractions in CommuniCore East – 141   Attractions in

CommuniCore West – 143   The Living Seas – 143   The Land – 145   *Journey into Imagination* – 147   The World of Motion – 150   Horizons – 151   Wonders of Life – 152   Universe of Energy – 154

World Showcase   156

Mexico – 156   Norway-157   People's Republic of China – 158   Germany – 159   Italy – 160   United States – 160   Japan – 161   Morocco – 162   France – 162   United Kingdom – 163   Canada – 163

EPCOT Center Ride Information   165

Cutting Down Your Time in Line by Understanding the Rides – 165

EPCOT Center Theater Information   166

Cutting Down Your Time in Line by Understanding the Shows – 166

Live Entertainment in EPCOT Center   167

Eating in EPCOT Center   169

Shopping in EPCOT Center   178

EPCOT Center One-Day Touring Plans   179

Traffic Patterns in EPCOT Center   180

EPCOT Center One-Day Touring Plan, for Adults   183

Outline of EPCOT Center One-Day Touring Plan, for Adults   189
Outline of EPCOT Center One-Day Touring Plan, for Parents with Small Children   191
Not to be Missed at EPCOT Center   192
Table Summary   194

PART FIVE—The Disney–MGM Studios and Studio Tour

And Now for Something Completely Different (Again) – 197   The MGM Connection – 197   Comparing Disney-MGM Studios to the Magic Kingdom and EPCOT Center – 197   How Much Time to Allocate – 198   Arriving and Getting Oriented – 199   What to See – 200

Open-Access/Movie Theme Park Section   201

Hollywood Boulevard – 201   Hollywood Boulevard Services – 201   The Great Movie Ride – 202   Disney Television Theater – 202   Star Tours – 203   Sound Effects Stage – 204   Epic Stunt Theater – 205

The Studio Tour 206
  The Walking Tour – 207
Eating at Disney-MGM Studios 208
Shopping at Disney-MGM Studios 208
Disney-MGM Studios One-Day Touring Plan 209

APPENDIX: Special Tours and Nightlife

Behind the Scenes Tours at Walt Disney World 213
Walt Disney World at Night 214
  Walt Disney World Dinner Theaters – 214   Other Area Dinner
  Theater Options – 216

Index 219

—— *Acknowledgments* ——

Special thanks to our field research team who rendered a Herculean effort in what must have seemed like a fantasy version of Sartre's *No Exit* to the tune of *It's a Small World*. We hope you all recover to tour another day.

Ray Westbrook
Joan W. Burns
Cyril C. Sehlinger
Pid Rafter
Karin Zachow
Paula Owens
Mary Mitchell

Many thanks also to Barbara Williams and Charles Ellertson for design and production, and to Carol Offen and Elizabeth Shoemaker for editorial work on this book. Tseng Information Systems earned our appreciation by keeping tight deadlines in providing the typography.

— The Unofficial Guide to
Walt Disney World®
& EPCOT® —

How Come "Unofficial"?

This guidebook represents the first comprehensive *critical* appraisal of Walt Disney World. Its purpose is to provide the reader with the information necessary to tour the Magic Kingdom and EPCOT Center with the greatest efficiency and economy, and with the least amount of hassle and standing in line. The authors of this guide believe in the wondrous variety, joy, and excitement of the Disney attractions. At the same time, we recognize realistically that Walt Disney World is a business, with the same profit motivations as businesses the world over.

In this guide we have elected to represent and serve you, the consumer. Its contents were researched and compiled by a team of evaluators who were, and are, completely independent of Walt Disney World and its parent corporation. If a restaurant serves bad food, or a gift item is overpriced, or a certain ride isn't worth the wait, we can say so, and in the process, hopefully make your visit more fun, efficient, and economical.

How This Guide Was Researched and Written

While much has been written concerning Walt Disney World, very little has been comparative or evaluative. Most guides simply parrot Disney World's own promotional material. In preparing this guide, however, nothing was taken for granted. Each theme park was visited at different times throughout the year by a team of trained observers. They conducted detailed evaluations and rated each theme park with all its component rides, shows, exhibits, services, and concessions according to a formal, pretested rating instrument. Interviews with attraction patrons were conducted to determine what tourists—of all age groups —enjoyed most and least during their Disney World visit.

While our observers were independent and impartial, we do not claim special expertise or scientific background relative to the types of exhibits, performances, or attractions. Like you, we visit Walt Disney World as tourists, noting our satisfaction or dissatisfaction. We do not believe it necessary then to be an agronomist to know whether we enjoyed the agricultural exhibits in the EPCOT Center Land pavilion. Disney offerings are marketed to the touring public, and it is as the public that we have experienced them.

The primary difference between the average tourist and the trained evaluator is in the evaluator's professional skills in organization, preparation, and observation. The trained evaluator is responsible for much more than simply observing and cataloging. While the tourist seated next to him is being entertained and delighted by the *Tropical Serenade (Enchanted Tiki Birds)* in the Magic Kingdom, the professional is rating the performance in terms of theme, pace, continuity, and originality. He or she is also checking out the physical arrangements: Is the sound system clear and audible without being overpowering; is the audience shielded from the sun or from the rain; is seating adequate; can everyone in the audience clearly see the staging area? And what about guides and/or performers: Are they knowledgeable, articulate,

4

and professional in their presentation; are they friendly and engaging? Does the performance begin and end on time; does the show contain the features described in Disney World's promotional literature? These and many other considerations figure prominently in the rating of any staged performance. Similarly, detailed and relevant checklists were prepared and applied by observer teams to rides, exhibits, concessions, and to the theme parks in general. Finally observations and evaluator ratings were integrated with audience reactions and the opinions of patrons to compile a comprehensive quality profile of each feature and service.

In compiling this guide, we recognize the fact that a tourist's age, sex, background, and interests will strongly influence his or her taste in Walt Disney World offerings and will account for a preference of one ride or feature over another. Given this fact we make no attempt at comparing apples with oranges. How indeed could a meaningful comparison be made between the priceless historic artifacts in the Mexican pavilion of EPCOT Center and the wild roller coaster ride of the Magic Kingdom's Space Mountain? Instead, our objective is to provide the reader with sufficient description, critical evaluation, and pertinent data to make knowledgeable decisions according to individual tastes.

The essence of this guide, therefore, consists of individual critiques and descriptions of each feature of the Magic Kingdom and EPCOT Center, and several detailed Touring Plans to help you avoid bottlenecks and crowds.

Walt Disney World—An Overview

If you are selecting among the tourist attractions in Florida, the question is not whether to visit Walt Disney World but how to see the best of the various Disney offerings with some economy of time, effort, and finances.

Make no mistake, there is nothing on earth quite like Walt Disney World. Incredible in its scope, genius, beauty, and imagination, it is a joy and wonder for people of all ages. A fantasy, a dream, and a vision all rolled into one, it transcends simple entertainment, making us children and adventurers, freeing us for an hour or a day to live the dreams of our past, present, and future.

Certainly we are critics, but it is the responsibility of critics to credit that which is done well as surely as to reflect negatively on that which is done poorly. The Disney attractions are special, a quantum leap beyond and above any man-made entertainment offering we know of. We cannot understand how anyone could visit Florida and bypass Walt Disney World.

—— What Walt Disney World Encompasses ——

Walt Disney World encompasses forty-three square miles, an area twice the size of Manhattan Island. Situated strategically in this vast expanse are two major theme parks, a filmmaking studio and tour (opening spring 1989), the world's largest swimming theme park (opening spring 1989), a smaller swimming attraction, a botanical and zoological exhibit, a nightlife entertainment area, several golf courses, hotels, four large interconnected lakes, a shopping complex, a convention center, a permanent nature preserve, and a complete transportation system consisting of four-lane highways, an elevated monorail, and a system of canals.

Most tourists refer to the entire Florida Disney facility as Walt Disney World, or more simply, as Disney World. The Magic Kingdom and EPCOT Center are thought of as being "in" Disney World. Other visitors refer to the Magic Kingdom as Disney World and EPCOT Center as EPCOT, and are not sure exactly how to label the entity as a whole. In our description we will refer to the total Disney facility as Walt Disney World according to popular tradition, and will consider the Magic Kingdom, EPCOT Center, and everything else that sits on that forty-three-square-mile chunk of real estate to be included in the overall designation.

The Major Theme Parks

The Magic Kingdom

The Magic Kingdom is what most people think of when they think of Walt Disney World. It is the collection of adventures, rides, and shows symbolized by the Disney cartoon characters and Cinderella Castle. Although the Magic Kingdom is only one element of the Disney attraction complex, it remains the heart of Disney World. The Magic Kingdom is divided into seven subareas or "lands," six of which are arranged around a central hub. First encountered is Main Street, U.S.A., which connects the Magic Kingdom entrance with the central hub. Moving clockwise around the hub, other lands are Adventureland, Frontierland, Liberty Square, Fantasyland, and Tomorrowland. Mickey's Birthdayland, the first new land in the Magic Kingdom since the park opened, is situated along the Walt Disney Railroad on three acres between Fantasyland and Tomorrowland. Access is through Fantasyland or via the railroad. Main Street and the other six lands will be described in detail later. Three hotel complexes (Contemporary Resort Hotel, Polynesian Village Resort, and the Grand Floridian Beach Resort) are located close to the Magic Kingdom and are directly connected to it by monorail and by boat.

EPCOT Center

EPCOT (Experimental Prototype Community of Tomorrow) Center opened in October of 1982. Divided into two major areas, Future World and World Showcase, the park is twice the size of and is comparable in scope to the Magic Kingdom. Future World consists of a number of futuristic pavilions, each relating to a different theme concerning man's creativity and technological advancement. World Showcase, arranged around a forty-one-acre lagoon, presents the architectural, social, and cultural heritages of almost a dozen nations, with each country represented by famous landmarks and local settings familiar to world travelers. EPCOT Center is generally more educationally oriented than the Magic Kingdom and has been repeatedly characterized as a sort of permanent world's fair. Unlike the Magic Kingdom, which Disney spokesmen represent as being essentially complete, EPCOT Center is pictured as a continually changing and growing entity. EPCOT Center is connected to the Magic Kingdom and resort hotels by monorail.

The Disney-MGM Studios (opens 1989)

This $300 million, 100-plus-acre attraction, which opens in 1989, is divided into two areas. The first is a theme park relating to the past, present, and future of the motion picture industry. This section contains movie-theme rides and shows and covers about a third of the Disney-MGM complex. Highlights here include a re-creation of Hollywood Boulevard from the 20s and 30s, audience participation shows on TV production and sound effects, movie stunt demonstrations, the Star Tours ride (opens 1990), and the Great Movie Ride, Disney's most ambitious ride-adventure, which takes guests for a journey through the movies' greatest moments.

The second area, encompassing the remaining two-thirds, is a working motion picture and television production facility comprised of three sound stages, a back lot of streets and sets, and creative support services. Access to this area is limited to the public except through studio tours which take visitors behind the scenes for a two-hour crash-course on movie making, including the opportunity to witness the actual shooting of feature films and television shows.

The Disney-MGM Studios are connected to other Walt Disney World areas by highway and canal, but not by monorail. Guests can park in the Studios' own pay parking lot or commute by bus from EPCOT Center, the Transportation and Ticket Center, or from any Walt Disney World lodging.

—— The Swimming Theme Parks ——

Typhoon Lagoon (opens spring 1989)

Designed to be the ultimate swimming theme park, Typhoon Lagoon is four times the size of River Country, Walt Disney World's first splash-and-sun attraction. Nine water slides and streams, some as long as 400 feet, drop from the top of a one-hundred-foot-high man-made mountain. Landscaping and an "aftermath of a typhoon" theme impart an added adventurous touch to the wet rides. Features include the world's largest inland surf facility, with waves up to six feet in height in a lagoon large enough to "encompass an oceanliner," and a saltwater snorkeling pool where guests can swim around with a multitude of real fish, including small sharks.

Beautifully landscaped, Typhoon Lagoon is entered through a misty rain forest emerging into a ramshackle tropical town where concessions and services are situated. Disney special effects make every ride an odyssey as swimmers encounter bat caves, lagoons and pools, spinning rocks, dinosaur bone formations, and countless other imponderables.

Typhoon Lagoon provides water adventure for all age groups. Activity pools for young children and families feature geysers, tame slides, bubble jets, and fountains. For the older and more adventurous there are two speed slides, three corkscrew body slides, and three tube/rapids rides (plus one children's rapids ride) plopping off Typhoon Mountain. For slower metabolisms there is Upalazy River, a scenic, relaxed, meandering, 2,100-foot-long tube ride that winds through a hidden grotto and a rain forest. And, of course, for the sedentary, there is usually plenty of sun to sleep in.

What sets Typhoon Lagoon apart from other water parks is not so much its various slides, but the Disney attention to detail in creating an integrated adventure environment. The eye (as well as the body) is deluged with the strange, the exotic, the humorous and the beautiful. In point of fact, faster, higher, and wilder slides and rapid rides can be found elsewhere. But no other water park comes close to Typhoon Lagoon in diversity, variety, adventure, and total impact.

Typhoon Lagoon has its own 1,000-car pay parking lot and can also be reached by shuttle bus from Walt Disney World and Walt Disney World Village hotels and campgrounds. There are no lodging accommodations at Typhoon Lagoon. Concessions include rental wetsuits, fins, snorkels, and underwater cameras for those who wish to swim with the fish at Shark Reef, surfing gear for the surfing lagoon, and two fast-food restaurants for the hungry. Facilities are ample with changing rooms, lockers, and showers, a lovely picnic area, and plentiful lounge chairs.

Typhoon Lagoon Touring Tips When it comes to water slides, unfortunately, modern traffic engineering bows to old-fashioned queuing theory. It's one person, one raft, or one tube at a time, and the swimmer "on deck" cannot go until the person preceeding him is safely out of the way. Thus the hourly carrying capacity of a slide is nominal compared to the continuously loading rides of EPCOT Center and the Magic Kingdom. Since a certain interval between swimmers is required for safety, there are only two ways to increase capacity: (1) make the watercourse longer so that more swimmers can safely be on the slide or rapids ride at the same time (Disney has done this—some slides approach 400 feet in length), and (2) increase the number of slides and rapids rides.

Though large and elaborate, Typhoon Lagoon actually has fewer slides than Wet and Wild (its main Orlando area competitor) and on crowded days long lines can develop for the chutes coming off Typhoon Mountain. Thus, to beat the crowd, we recommend arriving early (call the night before for opening time). Stake out some recliners in a spot you like and rent diving and/or surfing gear if you desire. Then, store your rental equipment and hit the slides and rapids rides until the crowds begin to build. When, as the park fills, the rides are no longer worth the wait, go on to dive at Shark Reef, ride Upalazy River, or surf in Typhoon Lagoon. Enjoy these attractions, the activity pools, a little lunch, and perhaps (heaven forbid) even a nap during the crowded heat of the day. If you are still around late in the afternoon, try the slides and rapids rides again.

The best way to avoid standing in lines is to visit Typhoon Lagoon on a day when it is less crowded. Because of the park's popularity among Florida locals, weekends can be tough. We recommend going on a Monday or Tuesday when most other tourists will be visiting the Magic Kingdom, EPCOT Center, or the Disney-MGM Studios, and the locals will be at work. Fridays are also a good bet since auto travelers commonly use this day to get a start on their trip home. Sunday morning is also a good time to go.

River Country

River Country is aesthetically among the best of the water theme parks—beautifully landscaped and immaculately manicured with rocky canyons and waterfalls skillfully blended with white sand beaches. The park is even situated to take advantage of the breeze blowing in from Bay Lake. For pure and simple swimming and splashing, River Country gets high marks. For its slides, however, River Country does not begin to compete with its big sister, Typhoon Lagoon, or with its nearby competitors. Where Wet and Wild (on International Boulevard) features in excess of 13 major slides and tube rides, River Country has one tube ride and two corkscrew-style slides. Few slides and many swimmers add up to long lines. If slides are your thing, and you are allergic to long lines, hit River Country as soon as it opens in the morning or alternatively in the hour before closing. You can come and go throughout the day simply by obtaining a reentry stamp.

Sunbathers will enjoy River Country, particularly if they position themselves near the lakefront to take advantage of any cooling breeze. Be forewarned, however, that the chaise lounges are basically flat with the head slightly elevated, and do not have adjustable backs. For a comfortable reading position or for lying on your stomach, therefore, they leave a great deal to be desired.

Access to River Country by car is a hassle. First you are directed to a parking lot ($2.50 per vehicle), where you leave your car, gather your personal belongings and wait for (what else?) a Disney tram to transport you to the water park. The tram ride is rather lengthy, and pity the poor soul who left his bathing suit in the car (a round-trip to retrieve it will take about a half hour).

There are no lodging accommodations at River Country. Food is available or you can pack in a picnic lunch to enjoy in River Country's picturesque, shaded lakeside picnic area. Access is by bus from the Transportation and Ticket Center (junction and transfer point for the EPCOT Center and Magic Kingdom monorails) or from the River Country parking lot on Vista Boulevard (see map, page 35). Combination passes, which include both River Country and Discovery Island, are available and represent the best buy for anyone interested in the minor Disney theme parks.

How Orlando/Kissimmee Area Water Theme Parks Stack Up

Just for the record, if you are into water theme parks, here's how the area's offerings compare:

	Typhoon Lagoon	River Country	Water Mania	Wet & Wild
Theme presentation	Yes	Yes	No	No
Beautiful scenery/landscaping	Yes	Yes	No	No
Large general swimming area	Yes	Yes	No	Yes
Children's swimming area	Yes	Yes	Yes	Yes

	Typhoon Lagoon	River Country	Water Mania	Wet & Wild
Snorkeling pool	Yes	Yes	Yes	Yes
Wave pool	Yes	No	Yes	Yes
Vertical-drop thrill slide	1	No	2	4
Graduated-drop thrill slide	1	No	2	2
Corkscrew body slide	3	2	3	3
Corkscrew tube/raft/mat slide	No	No	No	5
Whitewater rapids ride	4	1	No	1
Tranquil/scenic tube ride	1	No	No	1
Knee waterski	No	No	No	1

—— *The Minor Theme Parks* ——

Pleasure Island

Part of the Walt Disney World Village, Pleasure Island is a six-acre nighttime entertainment center where one cover charge will get a visitor into any of six nightclubs. The clubs are themed and feature a variety of shows and activities. There is roller skating, a comedy club, and a nonalcoholic club for those under 21. Music ranges from pop-rock to country and western. For the more sedentary (or exhausted) there is a ten-screen movie complex, or for the hungry, several restaurants.

Discovery Island

Situated in Bay Lake close to the Magic Kingdom, Discovery Island is a tropically landscaped, small zoological park primarily featuring birdlife. Small intimate trails wind through the exotic foliage, contrasting with the broad thoroughfares of the major theme parks. Plants and trees are marked for easy identification and the island features an absolutely enormous walk-through aviary, so cleverly engineered that you are essentially unaware of the confining netting. On the negative side, a trip to Discovery Island is fairly pricey (about $8) for a few birds and animals and a short stroll through the woods. As for children, they enjoy Discovery Island if allowed to explore on their own, but become bored and restless touring under the thumb of their elders. The best deal for seeing Discovery Island is to buy a River Country/Discovery Island combination ticket (about $15). But of

course it's only a good deal if you plan to go to both minor parks anyway. There are no lodging accommodations on Discovery Island, but
snacks are available. Access is exclusively by boat from the main Bay
Lake docks (Magic Kingdom Dock, Fort Wilderness Landing, Resort
Hotels' docks).

—— *Should I Go to Walt Disney World If I've Been to Disneyland in California?* ——

Walt Disney World is a much larger and more varied entertainment complex than is Disneyland. There is no EPCOT Center,
Disney-MGM Studios, or Typhoon Lagoon at Disneyland. To be specific, Disneyland is roughly comparable to the Magic Kingdom theme
park at Walt Disney World in Florida. Both the Magic Kingdom and
Disneyland are arranged by "lands" accessible from a central hub
and connected to the entrance by a Main Street. Both parks feature
many rides and attractions of the same name: Space Mountain, Jungle
Cruise, Pirates of the Caribbean, It's a Small World, and Dumbo, the
Flying Elephant, to name a few. Interestingly, however, the same name
does not necessarily connote the same experience. Pirates of the Caribbean at Disneyland is much longer and more elaborate than its Walt
Disney World counterpart. Space Mountain is far wilder in Florida,
and Dumbo is about the same in both places.

Disneyland is more intimate than the Magic Kingdom since it doesn't
have the room for expansion enjoyed by the Florida park. Pedes-
trian thoroughfares are more narrow, and everything from Big Thunder
Mountain to the Castle is scaled down somewhat. Large crowds are
less taxing at the Magic Kingdom since there is more room for them to
disperse.

At Disneyland, however, there are dozens of little surprises: small
unheralded attractions tucked away in crooks and corners of the park,
which give Disneyland a special charm and variety that the Magic
Kingdom lacks. And, of course, Disneyland has more of the stamp of
Walt Disney's personal touch.

For additional information on Disneyland, see *The Unofficial Guide
to Disneyland*, by Bob Sehlinger, Prentice Hall Press.

To allow for a meaningful comparison, we provide a summary of
those features found only at one of the parks, followed by a critical
look at the attractions found at both.

Attractions Found Only at the Magic Kingdom

Liberty Square:	*Hall Of Presidents*
Tomorrowland:	*Dreamflight*
	Carousel Of Progress
Mickey's Birthdayland:	All attractions

Attractions Found Only at Disneyland

Main Street:	*Great Moments With Mr. Lincoln*
Frontierland:	Sailing Ship Columbia
	Big Thunder Ranch
Fantasyland:	The Story of Sleeping Beauty
	Pinocchio's Daring Journey
	Casey Jr. Circus Train
	Storybook Land Canal Boats
	Alice In Wonderland
	Matterhorn Bobsleds
	Motor Boat Cruise
	Videopolis
Tomorrowland:	Star Tours
Bear Country:	Splash Mountain

Critical Comparison of Attractions Found at Both Parks

Main Street

WDW/Disneyland Railroad	The Disneyland Railroad is far more entertaining by virtue of the Grand Canyon Diorama and the Primeval World components not found at the Magic Kingdom.
The Walt Disney Story	More comprehensive film at the Magic Kingdom. More interesting static displays and memorabilia at Disneyland.

Adventureland

Jungle Cruise	More realistic AudioAnimatronic (robotic) animals at Walt Disney World, otherwise about the same.
Enchanted Tiki Room	About the same at both parks.
Swiss Family Treehouse	Larger at the Magic Kingdom.

New Orleans Square

Pirates of the Caribbean	Far superior at Disneyland.
Haunted Mansion	Slight edge to the Magic Kingdom version.

Bear Country

Country Bear Jamboree	Same production with much less of a wait at Disneyland.

Frontierland

Various river cruises (Canoes, steamboats, keelboats, etc.)	Slight edge to the Magic Kingdom in terms of the sights.
Tom Sawyer Island	Comparable, but a little more elaborate with better food service at the Magic Kingdom.
Big Thunder Mountain Railroad	Ride about the same. Sights and special effects better at the Magic Kingdom.
Golden Horseshoe Jamboree/Diamond Horseshoe Jamboree	Similar at both parks.

Fantasyland

Snow White's Scary Adventures	About the same at both parks.
Peter Pan's Flight	Better at Disneyland.
Mr. Toad's Wild Ride	Better at Disneyland.
Dumbo, the Flying Elephant	The same at both parks.
Carousels	About the same at both parks.
Castles	Far larger and more beautiful at the Magic Kingdom.
Mad Tea Party	The same at both parks.
It's a Small World	About the same at both parks.
Skyway	About the same at both parks.

Tomorrowland

Autopia/Grand Prix Raceway	About the same at both parks.

Mission to Mars	The same at both parks.
Rocket Jets/Starjets	The same at both parks.
PeopleMover	Edge to Disneyland.
World Premier Circle-Vision	The same at both parks.
Space Mountain	Vastly superior in terms of both ride and special effects at the Magic Kingdom.
Submarine Voyage/ 20,000 Leagues Under the Sea	About the same at both parks.

PART ONE—Planning
Before You Leave Home

—— Gathering Information ——

In addition to this guide, information concerning Walt Disney World can be obtained at the public library, through travel agencies, or by writing or calling:

Walt Disney World Company
Department GL, Box 10040
Lake Buena Vista, FL 32830-1000
Phone (407) 824-4321

Important Walt Disney World Telephone Numbers

General Information	(407) 824-4321
Reservations for Accommodations	(407) 824-8000
Magic Kingdom Lost & Found	(407) 824-4521
EPCOT Center Lost & Found	(407) 827-8236
Golf Tee Times	(407) 824-2270
Resort Dining and Recreation	
Information	(407) 824-3737
Walt Disney World Shopping Village	(407) 828-3058
Disney Car Care Center	(407) 824-4813
Childcare Information	(407) 827-5437

Closed for Repairs

It is always a good idea to check in advance with Walt Disney World to see which, if any, rides and attractions may be closed for maintenance or repair during your visit. If you are particularly interested in experiencing a particular attraction, this precautionary call could save you a lot of disappointment.

Timing Your Visit

—— *Trying to Reason with the Tourist Season* ——

It is one of the objectives of this book to assist the tourist, when possible, in avoiding crowds. It is useful therefore to understand the overall seasonality and traffic flow of Florida tourism.

Peninsular Florida (all of Florida except the Panhandle) has two peak seasons. One begins just before Christmas and ends just after Easter and is referred to as the "Winter Season" or sometimes just "the Season." The other, known as the "Summer Season" or "Family Season," gets into swing about the middle of June and lasts until late August.

Christmas Week, which effectively kicks off the Winter Season, is Florida's busiest week of the year, with facilities throughout the state (including attractions), being pushed to their limit. Many attractions offer special programs beginning several days prior to Christmas and extending through New Year's Day. Crowds, however, are awesome, with many smaller attractions inundated and long waits in line the norm at larger attractions. Because of the crowded conditions, we do not recommend Christmas Week for attraction touring. If, however, your schedule permits arriving the preceding week (say December 15th or thereabouts) crowds are manageable and sometimes even sparse. Get your touring in by the 22nd and then relax and enjoy the beach over Christmas.

Though the mammoth throngs of Christmas Week dissipate following New Year's Day, the Winter Season remains in full session with heavy attraction attendance through Easter. Easter Week is almost as congested as Christmas Week. During the Winter Season a high concentration of tourists is a fact of life.

The period between Easter and the beginning of the Summer Season in early June is usually slow and is a particularly good time for attraction touring. Activity picks up again toward the middle of June with the arrival of the family vacation traffic. This second season runs through late August when the kids return to school.

Attendance at individual attractions varies, with some attractions more popular with the Winter Season tourist and others more popular with the Summer Season tourist. This is attributable in part to the relatively small number of school-age children present during Winter Season.

September through mid-December is very slow throughout Florida except for the Thanksgiving holiday period. Our research team felt that the nicest time to visit Florida in terms of weather, low-stress touring, and crowd avoidance was the first two weeks in December, just prior to the Christmas crunch.

Holiday weekends throughout the year, as well as special events (Florida Derby, space craft launchings, auto races, local festivals, etc.) precipitate heavy attraction attendance in and out of season. On days immediately preceding or following the holiday periods, however, attendance is often extremely light.

The best weather in Florida usually occurs between late fall and mid-April, which coincides, of course, with the busy Winter Season. Attraction touring is pleasant throughout the day, though mornings and late afternoons are best for crowd avoidance during this time of the year.

During the warmer months of the Summer Season, comfort as well as crowd avoidance suggest early day touring.

Rainy days in both the Summer and Winter Seasons often afford excellent opportunities for beating the crowd. Many outdoor attractions offer good protection from the elements and are as enjoyable on a rainy day as on a sunny day. Indoor attractions see their heaviest attendance on rainy days. Here we recommend touring on sunny days during the very hot midday hours (11:30 A.M.–2:30 P.M.).

Off season (mid-April through early June and September through mid-December) touring is characterized by smaller crowds and by somewhat rainier weather, and is generally an excellent time to visit the state's premier, large-scale attractions. However, since attendance is lightest at these times it is not uncommon for certain major rides, shows, and exhibits to be closed for maintenance or revision. A phone call to the attraction under consideration will obtain information concerning which, if any, key features will be out of action during your intended visit.

The Florida Panhandle has a somewhat abridged Winter Season centered around Christmas and New Year's Day then followed by somewhat of a lull until March and April. The big season for the Panhandle is the Summer Season.

—— *Florida Traffic Patterns* ——

Attraction touring takes place both while traveling en route and at the tourist's vacation destination. Southern Florida is a destination area; tourists, upon arrival, visit local attractions as a supplement to their vacation itinerary. The Orlando area is both a vacation destination and an en route center of tourism. Many visitors spend their entire vacation in the Orlando area while others visit en route to or from southern Florida. Ocala by contrast is largely an en route center of tourism with most tourists stopping on their way to or from other destinations.

Since most tourists do their traveling to and from their vacation destination on weekends, it is possible to identify patterns of traffic which are useful in avoiding crowds. As an example, a Tennessee family whose primary destination is Walt Disney World may tour Silver Springs at Ocala en route. Departing Tennessee on Friday evening or Saturday morning places them at Silver Springs on Sunday, arriving in the Orlando area on Sunday evening. Since this is a very common itinerary, executed by thousands of tourists every week, a traffic pattern becomes discernible. Silver Springs will show its heaviest attendance on weekends. Walt Disney World, as a destination, will show large crowds on Monday, Tuesday, and Wednesday. Sea World, and other Orlando area attractions will see heavier attendance from Wednesday through Friday when visitors, such as our Tennessee family, have finished seeing the Magic Kingdom and EPCOT Center and begin to explore other attractions nearby.

Because of the extended driving distance, the average length of stay in Florida is greater for most tourists whose ultimate destination is southern Florida. An Ohio couple departing Columbus on Friday evening might typically tour St. Augustine or Marineland on Sunday and then proceed directly to their Fort Lauderdale destination or stop again for a day or two to tour Orlando area attractions. This itinerary places the couple at their Fort Lauderdale destination sometime late Monday, Tuesday, or Wednesday. Thus in southern Florida, attraction attendance is heaviest toward the end of the week and, as noted above,

Visitation patterns of specific centers of Florida tourism

Area	Tourism Classification	Heaviest Attendance	When to Go
Panhandle	Destination	Weekends	Weekdays
St. Augustine, Marineland	En route	Weekends	Weekdays
Ocala	En route	Weekends	Weekdays
Weeki Wachee, Homosassa Springs	En route	Weekends	Weekdays
Orlando, Cape Kennedy	En route, destination	Weekdays	Weekends
Tampa	En route, day trip from Orlando and from beaches	Thursday through Sunday	Monday through Wednesday
Clearwater, St. Petersburg	Destination	Winter: Sunday through Tuesday	Wednesday through Saturday
		Summer: Friday through Sunday	Monday through Thursday
Sarasota	En route, destination, day trip from beaches to the north	Varies	Varies
Naples, Bonita Springs	Destination	Varies	Varies
Southern Florida, East Coast	Destination	Thursday through Sunday	Monday through Wednesday
Keys, Key West	Destination, day trip from beaches to the north	Weekdays	Weekends

since visitors to southern Florida stay longer on the average, attendance remains heavy on weekends.

Thus, by understanding the more common patterns of arrival, departure, en route touring, and destination touring, it is possible to plan an attraction visitation itinerary which operates counter to the usual traffic flow and places the tourist at each chosen attraction on a day of lighter attendance.

Displayed above in summary form is a guide to the visitation patterns of specific centers of Florida tourism. Note that light and heavy attendance are relative terms, with light attendance in season possibly exceeding heaviest attendance out of season. Also remember that traffic patterns described are based on the norm, and that a specific day, according to the law of averages, will probably but not necessarily, approximate the norm.

When to Go to Walt Disney World

Selecting the Time of Year for Your Visit

Walt Disney World is busiest of all Christmas Day through New Year's Day. Thanksgiving weekend, the week of Washington's Birthday, spring break for colleges, and the two weeks around Easter are also extremely busy. To give you some idea of what busy means at Walt Disney World, up to 92,000 people have toured the Magic Kingdom alone on a single day! While this level of attendance is far from typical, the possibility of its occurrence should forewarn all but the ignorant and the foolish from challenging this mega-attraction at its busiest periods.

The least busy time of all is from after the Thanksgiving weekend until the week before Christmas. The next slowest times are September through the weekend preceding Thanksgiving, January 4th through the first half of February, and the week following Easter through early June. At the risk of being blasphemous, our research team was so impressed with the relative ease of touring in the fall and other "off" periods that we would rather take our children out of school for a week than do battle with the summer crowds.

Selecting the Day of the Week for Your Visit

A typical vacation scenario is for a family to arrive in the Orlando area on Sunday, visit the Magic Kingdom and EPCOT Center on Mon-

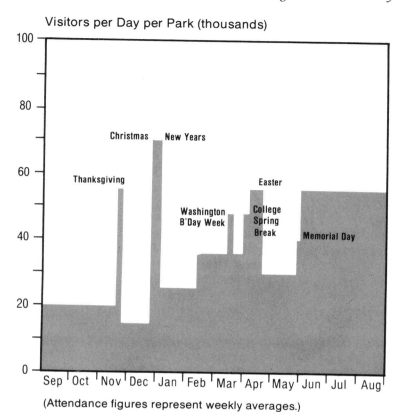

Visitors per Day per Park (thousands)

(Attendance figures represent weekly averages.)

day and Tuesday, visit Disney-MGM Studios on Wednesday, and go to Typhoon Lagoon or a non-Disney area attraction on Thursday. Friday is often reserved for heading home or to another Florida destination.

Given this often-repeated pattern, we recommend the following:

	Best Days to Go		Worst Days to Go	
Magic Kingdom & EPCOT Center	1	Friday	1	Monday
	2	Sunday	2	Tuesday
	3	Saturday (summer)	3	Wednesday
	4	Thursday		

	Best Days to Go		Worst Days to Go	
Disney-MGM Studios	1	Friday	1	Wednesday
	2	Sunday	2	Tuesday
	3	Saturday (summer)	3	Thursday
	4	Monday		
Typhoon Lagoon	1	Friday	1	Thursday
	2	Monday	2	Wednesday
	3	Tuesday	3	Saturday
	4	Sunday		

—— *Operating Hours* ——

It cannot be said that the Disney folks are not flexible when it comes to hours of operation for the parks. They run a dozen or more different operating schedules during the year, making it advisable to call (407) 824-4321 for the **exact** hours of operation the day before you arrive.

—— *Official Opening Time vs. Real Opening Time* ——

The hours of operation that the Disney folks will give you when you call are "official hours." In actuality the park will open earlier. If the official hours of operation are 9 A.M.–9 P.M., for example, the Main Street section of the Magic Kingdom will open at 8 or 8:30 A.M. and the remainder of the park will open at 8:30 or 9 A.M. Many visitors, relying upon the accuracy of the information disseminated by the Disney Guest Relations service, arrive at the stated opening time to find the park fairly thronged with people.

The Disney folks publish their hours of operation well in advance, but allow themselves the flexibility to react to gate conditions on a day-by-day basis. Based on a survey of local hotel reservations, Disney traffic controllers estimate how many visitors to expect on a given day. To avoid bottlenecks at the parking facilities or theme park ticket lines, the theme parks are frequently opened early, absorbing the crowds as they arrive.

We recommend arriving an hour before the official opening time at either EPCOT Center or the Magic Kingdom regardless of the time of year of your visit. If you happen to go on a major holiday, arrive an hour and twenty minutes in advance of the official opening time.

As concerns closing time, the Disney people usually close all rides and attractions at approximately the official stated closing time. Main Street in the Magic Kingdom remains open a half hour to an hour after the rest of the park has closed, as does the World Showcase section of EPCOT Center and Hollywood Boulevard at Disney-MGM Studios.

—— *Packed Park Compensation Plan* ——

The thought of teeming, jostling throngs jockeying for position in endless lines under the baking Fourth of July sun is enough to wilt the will and ears of the most ardent Mouseketeer. Why would anyone go to Walt Disney World during a major holiday period? Indeed, if you have never been to Walt Disney World, and you thought you would just drop in for a few rides and a little look-see on such a day, you might be better off shooting yourself in the foot. The Disney folks, however, being Disney folks, feel kind of bad about those long, long lines and the basically impossible touring conditions on packed days and compensate their patrons with a no-less-than-incredible array of first-rate live entertainment and happenings.

Throughout the day the party goes on with shows, parades, concerts, and pageantry. In the evening, particularly, there is so much going on that you have to make some tough choices. There are concerts, parades, light shows, laser shows, fireworks, and dance occurring almost continually in both parks. No question about it, you can go to Walt Disney World on the Fourth of July (or on any other extended hours, crowded day), never get on a ride, and still get your money's worth five times over. Admittedly, it's not the ideal situation for a first-timer who really wants to see the theme parks, but for anyone else it's one heck of a good party.

If you decide to go on one of the park's "big" days, we suggest that you arrive an hour and twenty minutes before the stated opening time. Use the Walt Disney World One-Day Touring Plan of your choice until about 1 P.M. and then take the Monorail to the Walt Disney World resort hotels for lunch and relaxation. Local Floridians visiting Walt Disney World on holidays often chip in and rent a room for the group (make reservations well in advance) in one of the Walt Disney World hotels, thus affording a place to meet, relax, have a drink, or change clothes prior to swimming. A comparable arrangement can be made at other nearby hotels as long as they furnish a shuttle service to and from the parks. After an early dinner, return to the park of your choice for the evening's festivities, which get cranked up about 8 P.M.

A Word About Lodging

While this guide is not about lodging, we have found lodging to be a primary concern of those visiting Walt Disney World. In general, and with one or two exceptions, rooms in hotels served by monorail are the most expensive, while rooms at other WDW hotel properties run slightly less. Least expensive are motels located outside of Walt Disney World.

In addition to proximity and a certain number of guest privileges, there is special magic and peace of mind associated with staying inside Walt Disney World. "I feel more a part of everything and less like a visitor," is the way one guest described it.

There is no real hardship, however, to staying outside Walt Disney World and driving (or taking the often available hotel shuttle) to the theme parks for your visit. Meals can be had less expensively, too, and there is this indirect benefit: rooming outside "The World" puts you in a more receptive mood towards other Orlando area attractions and eating establishments. Cypress Gardens, Busch Gardens, and Sea World, among others, are well worth your attention.

Prices for accommodations are subject to change, but our research team lodged in an excellent (though not plush) motel surrounded by beautiful orange groves for one quarter of the cost of staying in Walt Disney World. Our commuting time was 17 minutes one way to the Magic Kingdom or EPCOT Center parking lots.

—— Staying in the World* ——

Expensive, but most convenient, are the hotels situated around the Seven Seas Lagoon or Bay Lake and connected to the Magic Kingdom and EPCOT Center by monorail. These include the giant A-frame Contemporary Resort Hotel, the Polynesian Village Resort, and the

---

* Prices quoted are summer rates, double occupancy, and are subject to change.

new Grand Floridian Beach Resort, modeled after the fabled Florida beach resorts of the nineteenth century. Accommodations in any of these hotels make touring Walt Disney World easier and more relaxing. Commuting to and from the theme parks via monorail is quick and simple, allowing a visitor to return at leisure to his hotel for a nap or a dip. Additionally, the Seven Seas Lagoon and Bay Lake offer a variety of boating, swimming, and other water sports.

Contemporary Resort Hotel
1,050 rooms	lakefront	monorail service	$135–215 per night

Polynesian Village Resort
863 rooms	lakefront	monorail service	$135–220 per night

Grand Floridian Beach Resort
900 rooms	lakefront	monorail service	$165–265 per night

The Best Lodging Deal in Walt Disney World for the economy conscious is the new Caribbean Beach Resort. Situated on a 42-acre lake not far from EPCOT Center, the resort offers nightly rates of $75–$85. While it is not serviced by monorail, getting around Walt Disney World is easy via private car or Disney-provided shuttle buses.

Caribbean Beach Resort
2,112 rooms	lakefront	shuttle bus service	$65–85 per night

The Disney Inn (formerly the Golf Resort Hotel) which, in addition to being near the theme parks, offers 72 holes of golf. Walt Disney World transportation is by private car and shuttle bus.

The Disney Inn
288 rooms	golf course	shuttle bus service	$125–165 per night

The Walt Disney World Swan Resort, Dolphin Hotel, and Convention Center (opening 1990), is the largest convention/resort complex in the southeastern U.S. Built on the shore of a 50-acre lagoon, the complex is connected by canal to EPCOT Center and to the Disney-MGM Studios, as well as by highway to other areas of Walt Disney World. Expensive.

Swan Resort (opens 1989)
760 rooms	lakefront	boat/bus service	$135–265 per night

Dolphin Hotel (opens 1990)
1,510 rooms	lakefront	boat/bus service	$135–265 per night

Fort Wilderness Campground is a spacious resort campground for both tent and RV camping. Fully equipped, air-conditioned trailers are also available for rent. Aside from economy accommodations, features of Fort Wilderness Campground include full RV hookups, evening entertainment, a group camping area, horseback riding, bike trails, jogging trails, swimming, and a petting farm. River Country is situated near Fort Wilderness Campground. Access to the Magic Kingdom and Discovery Island is via boat from the Fort Wilderness landing on Bay Lake, or to any destination in Walt Disney World via private car or shuttle bus.

Fort Wilderness Campground

827 campsites	boat/bus service	$25–39 per night
363 trailers (sleeps 4–6)	boat/bus service	$130–145 per night

The Walt Disney World Village is about six minutes from EPCOT Center by car and close to I-4. A huge entertainment/dining/lodging/shopping complex, Walt Disney World Village offers a variety of lodging. The villas in Walt Disney World Village Resort are the only hotel accommodations in Walt Disney World proper which offer kitchen facilities. A not inexpensive grocery is conveniently located in the shopping complex.

Fairway Villas	64 units	bus service	$225–250 per night
Treehouse Villas	60 units	bus service	$250–275 per night
Vacation Villas	119 units	bus service	$175–250 per night
Club Lake Villas	324 units	bus service	$130–150 per night

Village Hotel Plaza. In addition to the Village Resort, seven hotels, offering a total of 3,605 rooms are situated in the Village Hotel Plaza. Although commodious, some rooms are more expensive than the Seven Seas Lagoon or Bay Lake hotels; we found few bargains in the Walt Disney World Hotel Plaza, and less of that special excitement you feel when you stay inside "The World." While technically part of Walt Disney World, the feel is different here, like visiting a colony instead of the mother country.

Grosvenor Resort	614 rooms	bus service	$90–120 per night
Buena Vista Palace	844 rooms	bus service	$110–179 per night
Hotel Royal Plaza	396 rooms	bus service	$127–160 per night
Howard Johnson's	383 rooms	bus service	$115–165 per night

The Hilton	814 rooms	bus service	$130–185 per night
Viscount Hotel	325 rooms	bus service	$139 per night
Pickett Suite Resort	229 rooms	bus service	$145–205 per night

—— *Lodging Outside of Walt Disney World* ——

Lodging costs outside Walt Disney World vary incredibly. If you shop around you can find a nice clean motel with a pool within twenty minutes of Walt Disney World for as low as $25 per night. There are five primary "out-of-the-World" areas to consider:

1. *International Drive area.* This area, about fifteen minutes east of Walt Disney World, parallels I-4 and offers a wide selection of both hotels and restaurants. Accommodations here range from $35–160 per night. Traffic here, however, is very congested.

2. *FL 192.* This is the highway to Kissimmee, southwest of Walt Disney World. There are many small, privately owned motels in this area offering good lodging value. Certain motels on FL 192 are as close to the Magic Kingdom as the more expensive hotels in the Walt Disney World Village Hotel Plaza. Rooms along FL 192 range from $25–140 per night.

3. *US 441, the Orange Blossom Trail.* Especially in the area where US 441 intersects Sand Lake Road, there are nice hotels and restaurants. This is an area where our research team enjoys staying because of the good local and chain restaurants. Driving time to Walt Disney World is about 15 minutes. Rates go from $30–90 per night.

4. *The I-4 corridor northeast of Walt Disney World.* There are a number of hotels situated on the north side of I-4 between Walt Disney World and Orlando which are convenient and reasonably priced ($40–110 per night).

5. *Downtown Orlando.* While requiring a half-hour commute to Walt Disney World, downtown Orlando offers some good lodging values. Since it markets its rooms more to business travelers than to tourists, you can often get a special deal at a very plush hotel on weekends.

There has been a tremendous amount of new lodging development in and around Walt Disney World. As more and more new rooms become available, the market will become much more competitive, and many of the hotels will have to offer discounted rates to keep their rooms filled. One way to discover these bargains is to check out the brochure racks at the Florida stateline welcome centers and at the service plazas on Florida's Turnpike.

Lodging Discounts in the Walt Disney World Area

A company called EIG (Exit Information Guide) publishes a book of discount coupons for bargain rates at hotels throughout the state of Florida. These books are available free of charge in many restaurants and motels along the main interstate highways leading to the Sunshine State. Since most folks make reservations prior to leaving home, picking up the coupon book en route does not help much. For one dollar, however, EIG will mail you a copy before you make your reservations. Write to:

Exit Information Guide
618 South Main Street
Gainesville, FL 32601

Getting There

Directions

If you arrive by automobile you can reach any Walt Disney World attraction or destination via World Drive, off US 192, or via EPCOT Center Drive, off I-4 (see map, page 35).

If you are traveling *south* on the Florida Turnpike: Exit at Clermont, take US 27 south, turn left onto US 192, and then follow the signs to Walt Disney World.

If you are traveling *north* on the Florida Turnpike: Exit westbound onto I-4 and exit I-4 at EPCOT Center Drive.

If you are traveling *west* on I-4: Exit at EPCOT Center Drive and follow the signs.

If you are traveling *east* on I-4: Exit to US 192 northbound and then follow the signs.

Walt Disney World Village has its own entrance separate and distinct from entrances to the theme parks. To reach Walt Disney World Village take FL 535 exit off of I-4 and proceed north, following the signs.

The Parking Situation

The Magic Kingdom and EPCOT Center have their own pay parking lots (each one the size of Vermont), including close-in parking for the handicapped. In the case of the Magic Kingdom, a tram meets you at a loading station near where you parked and transports you to the Transportation and Ticket Center. Here you can buy passes to both the Magic Kingdom and EPCOT Center. If you wish to proceed to the Magic Kingdom you can either ride the ferryboat across Seven Seas Lagoon or catch the monorail. If you wish to go to EPCOT Center, you can board a separate monorail that connects EPCOT Center to the Transportation and Ticket Center. The various sections of the Magic Kingdom (Transportation and Ticket Center) parking lot are named for

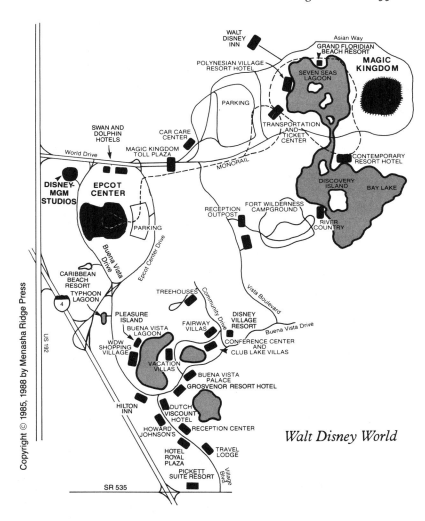

Walt Disney World

Disney characters. Guests are given a receipt with a map of the parking lot on the reverse side. Mark where you have parked on the map and jot down the aisle number in the space provided. Put the receipt in your billfold or some other safe place for referral when you return to your car. Failure to take these precautions will often result in a lengthy search for your car at a time when you will be pretty tuckered out.

If you wish to visit EPCOT Center you can park at the Magic Kingdom (Transportation and Ticket Center) parking lot and commute via monorail, or park directly in the EPCOT Center parking lot. Arrangements in the EPCOT Center lot are essentially the same as described above; a tram will shuttle you from where you park to the EPCOT Center entrance, and you will be given a receipt/map where you can mark your parking place for later reference. At EPCOT Center the sections of the parking lot are named for pavilions in the Future World area of the park. The big difference between parking for the Magic Kingdom and parking for EPCOT Center is that access to the park is direct from the tram at EPCOT Center whereas to reach the Magic Kingdom you must transfer from the tram to the ferryboat or the monorail at the Transportation and Ticket Center. If you park at EPCOT Center and wish to go to the Magic Kingdom you may do so by taking the monorail from EPCOT Center to the Transportation and Ticket Center and then transferring to a Magic Kingdom monorail.

Taking a Tram or Shuttle Bus from Your Hotel

Trams and shuttle buses are provided by many hotels and motels in the vicinity of Walt Disney World. They represent a fairly carefree alternative for getting to and from the theme parks, letting you off right at the entrance and saving you the cost of parking. The rub is that they might not get you there as early as you desire (a critical point if you take our touring advice) or be available at the time you wish to return to your lodging. Also, some shuttles go directly to Walt Disney World while others make stops at other motels and hotels in the vicinity. Each shuttle service is a little bit different so check out the particulars when you arrive at your hotel.

Disney-MGM Studios and Typhoon Lagoon Parking

Both the Disney-MGM Studios and Typhoon Lagoon will have their own pay parking lots with the familiar tram service to the door. Also available will be shuttle bus connections to the Transportation and Ticket Center and to the EPCOT Center parking lot. There is no monorail connection to either the studios or the swimming park.

Making the Most of Your Time

Allocating Time

During Walt Disney World's first decade, a family with a week's vacation could enjoy the Magic Kingdom and River Country and still have several days for the beach or other area attractions. Since the opening of EPCOT Center in 1982, however, Walt Disney World has steadily been enlarging to monopolize the same family's entire week. Today, with the additions of Typhoon Lagoon, the Disney-MGM Studios and Tour, and Pleasure Island, you had best allocate five days for a whirlwind tour (or seven days if you're old-fashioned and insist on a little relaxation during your vacation). If you do not have five or seven days, or think you might want to venture beyond the edge of "The World," be prepared to make some hard choices.

The theme parks, studios, and swimming attraction are **huge,** require a lot of walking, and sometimes a lot of waiting in lines. Moving in and among typically large crowds all day is exhausting. Oftentimes, the unrelenting central Florida sun zaps the most hearty traveler, making tempers short. In our many visits to Walt Disney World we observed, particularly on hot summer days, a dramatic transition from happy enthusiastic tourists upon arrival to zombies plodding along later in the day. Visitors who began their day enjoying the wonders of Disney imagination lapsed into an exhausted, production-line mentality ("We've got two more rides in Fantasyland, then we can go back to the hotel").

We recommend that you approach Walt Disney World the same way you would approach an eight-course Italian dinner: with plenty of time between courses. The best way not to have fun is to attempt to cram too much into too little time.

Prices Subject to Change Without Notice

Book reviewers who complain that prices quoted in guidebooks are out of date should note that Walt Disney World ticket prices seem to change about as often as the prime rate. If we were publishing a daily newspaper, maybe we could keep up. But since we are covering Walt Disney World in a book, we've decided to throw in the towel; no more listing admission prices. We will tell you this much, however: expect to pay a little under $30 for a 1-Day Ticket, a little under $80 for a 3-Day World Passport (there is no 2-Day admission), about $90 for a 4-Day World Passport, and about $110 for a 5-Day World Passport.

Walt Disney World Admission Options

There are basically two Walt Disney World admission options:

1. 1-Day Tickets
2. World Passports (3, 4, 5-Day and one year)

The 1-Day Magic Kingdom, EPCOT Center, or Disney-MGM Studios Ticket is good for one-day admission and unlimited use of "attractions and experiences" at the Magic Kingdom or EPCOT Center or the Disney-MGM Studios, but does not provide same-day admission to more than one of the three.

World Passports "entitle the visitor to admission plus unlimited use of attractions and experiences at the Magic Kingdom and EPCOT Center and Disney-MGM Studios. Includes transportation between all Vacation Kingdom resort areas. World Passports need not be used on consecutive days." With a World Passport you can tour the Disney-MGM Studios in the morning, stop by the Magic Kingdom for an afternoon parade, and have dinner at one of the ethnic restaurants in EPCOT Center that evening.

If you have only one day to spend, choose the park that most interests you and buy the 1-Day Ticket. If you have two days, you might want to go ahead and get the 3-Day World Passport. For the extra dollars you can visit both theme parks and the studios. At certain times of the year this will enable you to get in several extra hours of touring, since the parks do not always close at the same time. You will also have unlimited use of the monorail and shuttle systems.

If you plan to spend three days or more in the area, buy the 3-, 4-, or 5-Day World Passports. Remember, the passports do not have to be used on consecutive days. See *Optimum Touring Situation* below, for a relaxing, easygoing touring plan which makes use of this feature.

Which Park to See First:
The Magic Kingdom or EPCOT Center?

This question is less academic than it appears at first glance, especially if there are children or teenagers in your party. Children who see the Magic Kingdom first expect more of the same type of entertainment at EPCOT Center and are often disappointed by its educational orientation and more serious tone. In fact, many adults react exactly the same way.

For first-time visitors especially, see EPCOT Center first; you will be able to enjoy it fully without having been preconditioned to thinking of Disney entertainment as solely in the fantasy/adventure genre. Parties which include children should definitely see EPCOT Center first. Children will be more likely to judge and enjoy EPCOT Center according to its own merits if they see it first, as well as being more relaxed and patient in their touring.

—— *Optimum Touring Situation* ——

The optimum touring situation would call for having six days of touring time at your disposal. Buy the 5-Day World Passport. It entitles you to admission, plus unlimited use of attractions and experiences at both the Magic Kingdom and EPCOT Center, as well as at the Disney-MGM Studios. The World Passport does not have to be used on consecutive days.

Day One: Arrive at the EPCOT Center main parking lot forty-five minutes before the stated opening time. Line up at the turnstile to be admitted as soon as the park opens. When the gates open proceed posthaste to the Spaceship Earth attraction at the base of the giant geodesic dome (if you do not arrive before the gates open, bypass this attraction for the time being). If a sit-down lunch or dinner at a World Showcase restaurant is among your top priorities, save Spaceship Earth for later and go directly to one of the WorldKey Information touch-sensitive video screens (located directly across the lobby from the Spaceship Earth exit ramp) and make lunch and/or dinner reservations at the World Showcase restaurant of your choice. (See the descriptive text in the section on EPCOT Center for detailed information about EPCOT Center attractions and use of the WorldKey Information Service.)

After making lunch and/or dinner reservations tour The Living Seas, The Land pavilion, and then the Journey into Imagination pavilion. Eat as per your lunch reservations and then exit EPCOT Center for an afternoon of relaxing or whatever tickles your fancy. In the early evening return refreshed to EPCOT Center to eat dinner and to tour the remainder of the Future World section of the park.

Day Two: Arrive early and make dining reservations as on Day 1 if you wish to try additional World Showcase or Future World restaurants. Tour as tastes dictate in Future World, progressing to the World Showcase section of the park when it opens at 10 A.M. Follow World Showcase Descriptions and Touring Tips, pages 156–64. Finish touring and browse the shops in the early afternoon, or, if you make dinner reservations, exit EPCOT Center and tour Discovery Island, or take the afternoon off, returning at the appointed time for dinner.

Day Three: Tour the Magic Kingdom early in the morning when the lines are short and the day is cooler. At about noon go back to your hotel for lunch and maybe a swim or a nap, whatever you feel like.

If the Magic Kingdom closes early (6 P.M.–8 P.M.), return refreshed about two hours before closing and continue your visit in the relative cool and diminished crowds of the evening. Eat dinner somewhere outside of Walt Disney World after the Magic Kingdom closes, or if you still have some energy, ride the monorail over to EPCOT Center which almost always stays open later.

If the Magic Kingdom closes late (9 P.M.–1 A.M.), eat a relaxed dinner outside Walt Disney World and return refreshed to enjoy the Magic Kingdom until closing time.

Day Four: Finish touring the Magic Kingdom in the early morning. At about noon take the monorail to the Contemporary Resort Hotel for lunch. Return to the Magic Kingdom to browse the shops and take in the Disney character parades and other live shows which are performed in the early and mid-afternoon, and which require no waiting in line.

Try to complete your visit about four o'clock and head back to your hotel for happy hour and a little rest. Check before leaving the Magic Kingdom to see if there will be an evening performance of the Electrical Water Pageant on the Seven Seas Lagoon. If the answer is yes (and it usually will be), head for the dock at the Polynesian Village at the appointed time (just after dusk) for uncrowded enjoyment of the show. If you are an early diner, grab a bite outside Walt Disney World before returning for the Electrical Water Pageant. If you like a late dinner, indulge your palate after the show.

Day Five: If the weather is nice, head for Typhoon Lagoon at about 9:30 A.M. for a day of sun, swimming, and wet Disney adventures. Understand that Typhoon Lagoon is an event, a new wave (no pun intended) of Disney entertainment. Stated differently, do not forgo Typhoon Lagoon because you do not think you are the water park type. Like all Disney parks, there is something great here for everyone.

Having enjoyed Typhoon Lagoon to your satisfaction, head back to the hotel for some quiet time. In the evening after you have rested, explore the restaurants and nightlife at Pleasure Island. Once again, don't prejudge.

A final note on Day Five: Do not make any casual forays to EPCOT Center or the Magic Kingdom. You only have one day left on your World Passport, and you will need it for Day Six.

Day Six: Arrive at Disney-MGM Studios 35 minutes before the stated opening time. Upon entering, proceed down Hollywood Boulevard to the ornate gate at the end of the street. Take the combination tram and walking studio tour. After the tour, enjoy the various shows and attractions accessible from Hollywood Boulevard and around the lake.

Having enjoyed the studios to your satisfaction, use your World Passport to revisit the Magic Kingdom and/or EPCOT Center.

The essence of the preceding Optimum Touring Situation is to see the various attractions of Walt Disney World in a series of shorter, less exhausting visits during the cooler, less crowded parts of the day, with plenty of rest and relaxation in between visits. Since the Optimum Touring Situation calls for exiting and returning to the theme parks on most days it obviously makes for easier logistics if you are staying in or fairly close to Walt Disney World (twenty miles or less to your hotel). If you are lodged too far away for a great deal of coming and going, try relaxing during the heat of the day in the lounges or on the waterfronts of the Resort Hotels.

—— *Seeing Walt Disney World on a Tight Schedule* ——

Many visitors do not have four days to devote to Disney attractions. Some are en route to other Florida destinations while others wish to spend time sampling other central Florida attractions. For these visitors, efficient, time-effective touring is a must. They cannot afford long waits in line for rides, shows, or meals.

Even the most efficient touring plan will not allow the visitor to cover two or more of the major theme parks in one day, so plan on allocating at least an entire day to each attraction (an exception to this rule is when the theme parks close at different times, allowing the visitor to tour one park until closing time and then proceed to the other park). If your schedule permits only one day of touring overall, we recommend concentrating your efforts on only one of the theme parks and saving the other for a subsequent visit.

One-Day Touring

A comprehensive tour of the Magic Kingdom, EPCOT Center, or the Disney-MGM Studios in one day is possible but requires a knowledge of the park, good planning, and no small reserve of energy and endurance. One-day touring does not leave much time for leisurely meals in sit-down restaurants, prolonged browsing in the many shops, or lengthy rest periods. Even so, one-day touring can be a fun, rewarding experience.

Successful one-day touring of either the Magic Kingdom or EPCOT Center, or of the Disney-MGM Studios, hinges on **three cardinal rules**:

1. *Determine in Advance What You Really Want to See*

What are the rides and attractions that appeal to you most? Which additional rides and attractions would you like to experience if you have any time left? What are you willing to forgo?

2. *Arrive Early! Arrive Early! Arrive Early!*

This is the single most important key to efficient touring and avoiding long lines. First thing in the morning there are no lines and relatively few people. The same four rides which you can experience in one hour in the early morning will take more than three hours to see after 11:30 A.M. Have breakfast before you arrive so you will not have to waste your prime touring time sitting in a restaurant.

Always call the park, (407) 824-4321, the day before you visit to inquire at what time the park will open and close.

For the Magic Kingdom: Arrive at the main parking lot an hour before the stated opening time of the park (the parking lot and Transportation and Ticket Center open two hours early), buy your admission pass and take the monorail to the Magic Kingdom. You will find that Main Street, U.S.A. opens a half hour to an hour before the stated opening time of the park. Tour Main Street and be ready to see the other theme areas when they open.

For EPCOT Center: Arrive at the main parking lot forty-five minutes before the stated opening time. Buy your admission pass and line up at the turnstile to be admitted as soon as the park opens. EPCOT Center sometimes opens a half hour earlier than the stated opening time.

For Disney-MGM Studios: Arrive at the Studios parking lot 45 minutes before the stated opening time. Buy your admission and be ready to go. Hollywood Boulevard opens a half hour before the rest of the Studios.

Taking our advice about arriving early will work in your favor most of the time, particularly if you are vacationing at Disney World over any holiday period (including American Education Association or spring break), or during the summer. Because Disney opening procedures are flexible, however, you may occasionally suffer a few extra minutes of waiting to be admitted. Rest assured that this investment in time is more than worth it, once you pass through the turnstiles.

The Disney folks vary opening procedures according to the number of visitors they anticipate on a given day. Simply stated, they open up as early as required to avoid crowds overwhelming the parking facilities, ticket sellers, and transportation systems. On busier days this almost always translates into admitting visitors a half hour to an hour before the officially stated opening time.

3. Avoid Bottlenecks

Helping you avoid bottlenecks is what this guide is all about. Bottlenecks occur as a result of crowd concentrations and/or less than optimal crowd management. Concentrations of hungry people create bottlenecks at restaurants during the lunch and dinner hours; concentrations of people moving towards the exit near closing time create bottlenecks in the gift shops en route to the gate; concentrations of visitors at new and unusually popular rides create bottlenecks and long waiting lines; rides which are slow in boarding and disembarking passengers create bottlenecks and long waiting lines. Avoiding bottlenecks involves being able to predict where, when, and why they occur. To this end we provide **Touring Plans** for the Magic Kingdom, EPCOT Center, and the Disney-MGM Studios, as well as Touring Tips for Typhoon Lagoon, to assist you in avoiding bottlenecks. In addition we provide detailed information on all rides and performances which allows you to estimate how long you may have to wait in line, and it also allows you to compare rides in terms of their capacity to accommodate large crowds. Touring Plans for the Magic Kingdom begin on page 114, Touring Plans for EPCOT Center begin on page 179, Touring Plans for Disney-MGM Studios begin on page 209, and Touring Tips for Typhoon Lagoon begin on page 9.

—— Touring Plans: What They Are and How They Work ——

When we interviewed Walt Disney World visitors who toured the theme park on slow days, say in early December, they invariably waxed eloquent about the sheer delight of their experience. When we questioned visitors who toured on a moderate or busy day, however, they spent much of the interview telling us about the jostling crowds and how much time they stood in line. What a shame, they said, that you should devote so much time and energy to fighting the crowds in a place as special as Walt Disney World.

Given this complaint, we descended on Walt Disney World with a team of researchers to determine whether a touring plan could be devised that would move the visitor counter to the flow of traffic and allow him to see any of the theme parks in one day with only minimal waits in line. On some of the busiest days of the year, our team monitored traffic flow into and through the theme parks, noting how the parks filled and how the patrons were distributed among the various attractions. Likewise, we observed which rides and attractions were most popular and where bottlenecks were most likely to form.

After many long days of collecting data, we devised a number of preliminary touring plans which we tested during one of the busiest weeks of the entire year. Each day individual members of our research team would tour the park according to one of the preliminary plans, noting how long it took to walk from place to place and how long the wait in line was for each ride or show. Combining the knowledge gained through these trial runs, we devised a master plan which we retested and fine-tuned. This plan, with very little variance from day to day, allowed us to experience all of the major rides and attractions, and most of the lesser ones, in one day, with an average wait in line at each ride or show of less than five minutes.

From this master plan we developed a number of alternative plans that take into account the varying tastes and personal requirements of different Walt Disney World patrons. We devised a plan, for instance, for more mature guests that bypasses roller-coaster-type rides and requires less walking. Another plan was assembled for parents touring with children under the age of eight years. Each plan operates with the same efficiency as the master plan but addresses the special needs and preferences of its intended users.

Finally, after all of the plans were tested by our staff, we selected (using convenience sampling) a number of everyday Walt Disney World patrons to test the plans. The only prerequisite for being chosen for the test group (the visitors who would test the touring plans) was that the guest must be visiting a Disney attraction for the first time. A second group of ordinary patrons was chosen for a "control group," first-time visitors who would tour the park according to their own plans but who would make notes of what they did and how much time they spent waiting in lines.

When the two groups were compared, the results proved no less than amazing. On days when each park's attendance exceeded 48,000, visitors touring on their own (without the plan) **averaged** 3⅔ hours more waiting in line per day than the patrons touring according to our plan, and they experienced 37 percent fewer rides and attractions.

Will the Plans Continue to Work Once the Secret Is Out?

Yes! First, all of the plans require that a patron be on hand when the theme parks open. Many vacationers simply refuse to make this early-rising sacrifice, but you can see more in the one hour just after the parks open than in several hours once the parks begin to fill. Second, it is anticipated that less than I percent of any given day's attendance will have been exposed to the plans, not enough to bias the results. Last, most groups will interpret the plans somewhat, skipping certain rides or shows as a matter of personal taste.

Variables That Will Affect the Success of the Touring Plans

How quickly you move from one ride to another, when and how many refreshment and restroom breaks you take, when, where, and how you eat meals, and your ability (or lack thereof) to find your way around will all have an impact on the success of the plans. We recommend continuous, expeditious touring until around 11:30 A.M. After that hour, breaks and so on will not affect the plans significantly.

Some variables that can have a profound effect on the touring plans are beyond your control. Chief among these are the manner and timing of bringing a particular ride to full capacity. For example, Big Thunder Mountain, a roller coaster in the Magic Kingdom, has five trains. On a given morning it may begin operation with two of the five, and then add the other three if and when needed. If the waiting line builds rapidly before the Disney operators decide to go to full capacity, you could have a long wait, even early in the morning. This often happens at 20,000 Leagues Under the Sea, also in the Magic Kingdom, causing our team to label the ride as the biggest bottleneck in "the World."

Another variable relates to the time that you arrive for a Disney theater performance. Usually, your wait will be the length of time from your arrival to the end of the presentation then in progress. Thus, if *Country Bear Jamboree* is 15 minutes long, and you arrive one minute after a show has begun, your wait for the next show will be fourteen minutes. Conversely, if you happen to arrive just as the ongoing show is wrapping up, your wait will be only a minute or two. It's luck of the draw.

General Overview

The Walt Disney World Touring Plans are step-by-step plans for seeing as much as possible in one day with a minimum of time wasted standing in line. They are designed to assist you in avoiding crowds and bottlenecks on days of moderate to heavy attendance. On days of lighter attendance (see "Selecting the Time of Year for Your Visit," page 24), the plans will still save you time but will not be as critical to successful touring.

—— *Letters, Comments, and Questions from Readers* ——

Many of those who use *The Unofficial Guide to Walt Disney World* write to us asking questions, making comments, or sharing their own strategies for visiting Walt Disney World. We appreciate all such input, both positive and critical, and encourage our readers to continue writing. Readers' comments and observations are frequently incorporated in revised editions of *The Unofficial Guide* and have contributed immeasurably to its improvement.

How to Write the Authors

Bob Sehlinger & John Finley
The Unofficial Guide to Walt Disney World
Post Office Box 59257
Birmingham, AL 35259

—— *Walt Disney World Vacations Guided by the Authors* ——

The authors spend several weeks each year at Walt Disney World updating *The Unofficial Guide*. Twice annually, in March and in July, and on a limited basis, readers are invited to purchase a special tour package to Walt Disney World. On the tour, under the direction of the authors, they will enjoy the Walt Disney World vacation of a lifetime while assisting the research team in revising and improving the guide. The package is administered by an independent tour wholesaler and includes lodging, admissions, materials, and an itinerary developed and hosted by the authors. Airfare and rental car are optional. Interested parties should write:

Unofficial Guide to Walt Disney World
Special Tour & Research Week
c/o Western Leisure, Inc.
142 East 200 South, Suite 202
Salt Lake City, Utah 84111

PART TWO—Tips and Warnings

—— Credit Cards ——

- MasterCard, VISA, and American Express are accepted for theme park admission.
- No credit cards are accepted in the theme parks at fast-food restaurants.
- Walt Disney World shops, sit-down restaurants, and Theme Resort Hotels will accept MasterCard, VISA, and American Express credit cards only.

—— Rain ——

If it rains, go anyway; the bad weather will serve to diminish the crowds. Additionally, most of the rides and attractions are under cover. Likewise, all but a few of the waiting areas are protected from inclement weather.

—— Small Children ——

We believe that children should be a fairly mature eight years old to really *appreciate* the Magic Kingdom, though children of almost any age will *enjoy* it.

We believe that much of value at EPCOT Center will be lost on children less than ten years old, although children five years and older will be able to enjoy many specific features.

Small children often become tired and irritable after several hours of standing in line and being jostled among the crowds. If your schedule allows, we recommend small doses at a time of both the Magic Kingdom and EPCOT Center. Go early in the morning to the park of your choice and tour until about lunch time. Go back to your hotel for some food and maybe a nap. Return later in the evening or the morning of the following day.

There is more than enough action and excitement at the Disney-MGM Studios to keep small ones entertained, though they might not understand everything that is going on. Be mindful, however, that the special effects are more real and the monsters "badder" at the Studios. Children who frighten easily may have a few anxious moments.

Strollers—are available at a modest fee at all three theme parks. For infants and nonwalking toddlers the strollers are a must. We observed several sharp parents renting strollers for somewhat older children (up to 4 or 5 years). Having the stroller precluded having to carry children when they ran out of steam, and also afforded a place for children to sit during long waits in line. Strollers can be obtained at the right of the entrance to the Magic Kingdom (at the base of the Main Street Station) and on the left side of the Entrance Plaza of EPCOT Center. At the Disney-MGM Studios, stroller rentals are situated to the right of the entrance at Oscar's Super Service.

NOTE: Sometimes strollers disappear while you are enjoying a ride or a show. Do not be alarmed. You will not have to buy the missing stroller and you will be issued a new stroller for your continued use.

Baby-Sitting. If you are staying in one of the Theme Resort Hotels, you can contract for a baby-sitter to watch the kids in your hotel room. If you are staying anywhere on Walt Disney World property, including the Fort Wilderness Campground or the non-Disney-owned hotels at Walt Disney World Village, you can arrange for your children to be cared for at the Kindercare facility located at the Walt Disney World Village. For rates and other vital information call (407) 827-5437. Many of the larger motels and hotels outside of Walt Disney World also offer some sort of baby-sitting service; inquire when you make your reservations.

Caring for Infants and Toddlers. Both the Magic Kingdom and EPCOT Center have special centralized facilities for the care of infants and toddlers. Everything necessary for changing diapers, preparing formulas, warming bottles and food, etc., is available in ample quantity. A broad selection of baby supplies is on hand for sale and there are even rockers and special chairs for nursing mothers. In the Magic Kingdom the Baby Center is located next to the Crystal Palace at the end of Main Street. At EPCOT Center, Baby Services is located near the Odyssey Restaurant, situated to the right of the World of Motion in Future World. At Disney-MGM Studios, Baby Care is located in the Guest Relations complex to the left of the entrance.

Lost Children—normally do not present much of a problem at either theme park. All Disney employees are schooled to handle the situation should it be encountered. If you lose a child in the Magic Kingdom, report the situation to a Disney employee, and then check in at the Baby Center and at City Hall where lost-children "logs" are maintained. At EPCOT Center the procedure is the same; report the child lost and then check at Baby Services near the Odyssey Restaurant. At Disney-MGM Studios, report the child lost at the Guest Relations complex at the entrance end of Hollywood Boulevard. Paging systems are not used in any of the parks, but in an emergency, an "all points bulletin" can be issued throughout the park(s) via internal communications. At both theme parks, special name tags can be obtained to aid identification should a child become separated from his party.

Disney, Kids, and Scary Stuff.   Disney rides and shows are adventures. They focus on the substance and themes of all adventure, and indeed of life itself: good and evil, quest, death, beauty and the grotesque, fellowship and enmity. As you sample the variety of attractions at Walt Disney World, you transcend the mundane spinning and bouncing of midway rides to a more thought-provoking and emotionally powerful entertainment experience. Though the endings are all happy, the impact of the adventures, with Disney's gift for special effects, is often intimidating and occasionally frightening to small children.

There are rides with menacing witches, rides with burning towns, and rides with ghouls popping out of their graves, all done tongue-in-cheek and with a sense of humor, providing you are old enough to understand the joke. And bones, lot of bones: human bones, cattle bones, dinosaur bones, and whole skeletons everywhere you look. There have got to be more bones at Walt Disney World than at the Smithsonian Institute and Tulane Medical School combined. There is a stack of skulls at the headhunter's camp on the Jungle Cruise; a veritable platoon of skeletons sailing ghost ships in Pirates of the Caribbean; a haunting assemblage of skulls and skeletons in the Haunted Mansion; and more skulls, skeletons, and bones punctuating Snow White's Scary Adventures, Peter Pan's Flight, and Big Thunder Mountain Railroad, to name a few.

It should be mentioned that the monsters and special effects at the Disney-MGM Studios are more real and sinister than those of the other theme parks. If your child is having difficulty coping with the witch in Snow White's Scary Adventures, think twice about exposing him to machine-gun battles, earthquakes, and the creature from *Alien* at the Studios.

Most small children take Disney's variety of macabre trappings in stride, and others are quickly comforted by an arm around the shoulder or a little squeeze of the hand. But for those kids whose parents have observed a tendency to become upset when exposed to such sights, we recommend taking it slow and easy, sampling more benign adventures like the Jungle Cruise, gauging reactions, and discussing with children how they felt about the things they saw.

—— *Visitors with Special Needs* ——

Handicapped visitors—will find rental wheelchairs available if needed. Most rides, shows, attractions, restrooms, and restaurants at both theme parks are designed to accommodate the handicapped. For specific inquiries or problems call (407) 824-4321. If you are in the Magic Kingdom and need some special assistance go to City Hall on Main Street. At EPCOT Center, inquire at the Guest Relations booth in Earth Station at the base of Spaceship Earth. At Disney-MGM Studios, assistance can be obtained at Guest Relations to the left of the main entrance on Hollywood Boulevard.

Close-in parking is available for handicapped visitors at all Walt Disney World parking complexes. Simply request directions when you pay your parking fee upon entering. All monorails and most rides, shows, restrooms, and restaurants can accommodate wheelchairs. One major exception is the Contemporary Resort Hotel monorail station, where passengers must enter or exit via escalators.

A special information booklet for handicapped guests is available at wheelchair rental locations throughout Walt Disney World.

Foreign language assistance is available throughout Walt Disney World. Inquire by calling (407) 824-4321 or by stopping at City Hall in the Magic Kingdom, Earth Station Guest Relations at EPCOT Center, or at Hollywood Boulevard Guest Relations at the Disney-MGM Studios.

Messages can be left at City Hall in the Magic Kingdom, Earth Station Guest Relations at EPCOT Center, or at Hollywood Boulevard Guest Relations at the Disney-MGM Studios.

Car Trouble. If your car goes on the fritz, the Disney Car Care Center will come to the rescue. Arrangements can be made for transportation to your Walt Disney World destination and for a lift to the Car Care Center. If the problem is simple, one of the security or tow truck patrols which continually cruise the parking lots might be able to put you back in business.

Lost and Found. If you lose (or find) something in the Magic Kingdom, City Hall (once again) is the place to go. At EPCOT Center the Lost and Found is located in the Entrance Plaza, and at Disney-MGM Studios it is located at Hollywood Boulevard Guest Relations. If you do not discover your loss until you have left the park(s), call (407) 824-4245 (for all parks).

—— *Excuse Me, but Where Can I Find . . .* ——

Someplace to Put All These Packages? Lockers are available on the ground floor of the Main Street Railroad Station in the Magic Kingdom, to the right of Earth Station in EPCOT Center, and on both the east and west ends of the Ticket and Transportation Center. At Disney-MGM Studios, lockers are to the right of the entrance on Hollywood Boulevard.

A Mixed Drink or a Beer? If you are in the Magic Kingdom you are out of luck. You will have to exit the park and proceed to one of the Resort Hotels. In EPCOT Center you can have a drink, but you may need a reservation. Alcoholic beverages are served primarily in full-service eateries, although beer is available at the Cantina de San Angel opposite the Mexican pavilion; at Le Cellier, a cafeteria on the lower right side of the Canadian pavilion; and at the pub section of the Rose and Pub Dining Room in the Great Britain complex. The latter is popular not only because of the availability of beer, but also because of its unparalleled view of the World Showcase Lagoon. Finally, beer is also available at Yakatori House, the fast-food eatery in the Japanese pavilion. At Disney-MGM Studios, beer and wine are available at the Soundstage and Backlot restaurants.

Some Rain Gear? If you get caught in a central Florida monsoon, here's where you can find something to cover up with:

Magic Kingdom

Main Street:	The Emporium
Tomorrowland:	Mickey's Mart
Fantasyland:	Mad Hatter
	AristoCats
Frontierland:	Frontier Trading Post
Adventureland:	Tropic Toppers

EPCOT Center:	Almost all retail shops.
Disney-MGM Studios:	Almost all retail shops.

At Disney-MGM Studios and EPCOT Center shops rain gear is available but not always displayed. As the Disney people say, it is sold "under the counter." In other words, if you do not see it, ask for it.

A *Cure for This Headache?* Aspirin and various other sundries can be purchased on Main Street in the Magic Kingdom at the Emporium (they keep them behind the counter so you have to ask), at most retail outlets in EPCOT Center Future World, and in many of the World Showcase shops. Likewise at the Disney-MGM Studios, aspirin is available at almost all retail shops.

A *Prescription Filled?* Unfortunately there is no place in Walt Disney World to have a prescription filled.

Suntan Lotion? Suntan lotion and various other sundries can be purchased on Main Street in the Magic Kingdom at the Emporium (they keep them behind the counter so you have to ask), at most retail outlets in EPCOT Center Future World, and in many of the World Showcase shops. At the Disney-MGM Studios, suntan lotion is sold at almost all retail shops.

A *Smoke?* Cigarettes are readily available throughout both the Magic Kingdom and EPCOT Center.

Magic Kingdom

Main Street:	The Tobacconist
Tomorrowland:	Mickey's Mart
Fantasyland:	Royal Candy Shop
	Pinocchio Village Haus (vending machine)

King Stefan's in Cinderella Castle (vending machine)

Liberty Square:	Columbia Harbor House (vending machine)
	Heritage House
Frontierland:	Frontier Trading Post
	Mile Long Bar (vending machine)
Adventureland:	Tropic Toppers

EPCOT Center: Cigarettes are available at most Future World retail outlets and can be located in at least one of the shops in each of the World Showcase pavilions. Special imported cigarettes are additionally available at the British, French, and German pavilions.

Disney-MGM Studios: Under the counter at all stores.

Feminine Hygiene Products?   Feminine hygiene products are available in women's restrooms throughout Walt Disney World.

Cash?   Branches of the Sun Bank are located respectively on Main Street in the Magic Kingdom, on Hollywood Boulevard at the Disney-MGM Studios, and to the left of the turnstiles as you enter EPCOT Center. All branches offer the following services:

— *Provide cash advances on MasterCard and VISA* credit cards ($50 minimum with a maximum equaling the patron's credit limit).

— *Cash personal checks* of $25 and less drawn on US banks upon presentation of a valid driver's license and a major credit card.

— *Cash and sell traveler's checks*. Provide refunds for lost American Express traveler's checks.

— *Facilitate the wiring of money* from the visitor's bank to the Sun Bank.

— *Exchange foreign currency* for dollars.

Exchange My Foreign Currency?   The currency of most countries can be exchanged for dollars before you enter the theme parks, at the Guest Relations window of the Ticket and Transportation Center, the Guest Relations window in the ticketing area of the Disney-MGM Studios, and at the Guest Relations window to the right of the entrance turnstiles at EPCOT Center.

Leave My Pet? Cooping up an animal in a hot car while you tour can lead to disastrous results. Additionally, pets are not allowed in the major or minor theme parks. Kennels and holding facilities are provided for the temporary care of your pets, and are located adjacent to the Transportation and Ticket Center and to the left of the EPCOT Center Entrance Plaza. If you are adamant, the folks at the kennels will accept custody of just about any type of animal, though owners of exotic and/or potentially vicious pets must place their charge in the assigned cage. Small pets (mice, hamsters, birds, snakes, turtles, alligators, etc.) must arrive in their own escape-proof quarters.

In addition to the above, there are several other details that you may need to know:

— Advance reservations for animals are not accepted.

— Kennels open one hour before the theme parks open and close one hour after the theme parks close.

— Only Walt Disney World Resort guests may board a pet overnight.

— Guests leaving exotic pets should supply food for their pet.

Film? Camera centers are located near the Journey into Imagination pavilion and Spaceship Earth and at other shops throughout EPCOT Center. In the Magic Kingdom, film may be found at the Kodak Camera Center on Main Street, U.S.A., as well as at other shops throughout the park. At Disney-MGM Studios, film is available at most retail shops.

PART THREE—
The Magic Kingdom

Arriving and Getting Oriented

Both the ferryboat and the monorail discharge passengers at the entrance to the Magic Kingdom—the Train Station at the foot of Main Street. Stroller and wheelchair rentals are to the right, lockers for your use are on the ground floor of the Train Station. Entering Main Street, City Hall is to your left, serving as the center for information, lost and found, some reservations, and entertainment.

If you haven't been given a guide to the Magic Kingdom by now, City Hall is the place to pick one up. The guide contains maps, gives tips for good photos, lists all the attractions, shops, and eating places, and provides helpful information about first aid, baby care, assistance for the handicapped, and more.

While at City Hall inquire about special events, live entertainment, Disney character parades, concerts, and other activities scheduled for that day. Sometimes City Hall will have a printed schedule of the day's events; other days no printed handouts are available and you will have to take a few notes.

Notice from your map that Main Street ends at a central hub, from which branch the entrances to five other sections of the Magic Kingdom: Adventureland, Frontierland, Liberty Square, Fantasyland, and Tomorrowland. Mickey's Birthdayland is wedged like a dimple between the cheeks of Fantasyland and Tomorrowland, and does not connect to the central hub.

Cinderella Castle serves as the entrance to Fantasyland and is the focal landmark and visual center of the Magic Kingdom. If you start in Adventureland and go clockwise around the Magic Kingdom, the castle spires will always be roughly on your right; if you start in Tomorrowland and go counterclockwise through the park, the spires will always be roughly on your left. Cinderella Castle is a great place to meet if your group decides to split up for any reason during the day, or as an emergency meeting place if you are accidentally separated.

Starting the Tour

Everyone will soon find his own favorite and not-so-favorite attractions in the Magic Kingdom. Be open-minded and adventuresome. Don't dismiss a particular ride or show as being not for you until **after** you have tried it. Our personal experience as well as our research indicates that each visitor is different in terms of which Disney offerings he most enjoys. So don't miss seeing an attraction because a friend from home didn't like it; that attraction may turn out to be your favorite.

We do recommend that you take advantage of what Disney does best—the fantasy adventures like the Jungle Cruise and the Haunted Mansion, and the AudioAnimatronics (talking robots, so to speak) attractions such as the *Hall of Presidents* and Pirates of the Caribbean. Unless you have almost unlimited time, don't burn a lot of daylight browsing through the shops. Except for some special Disney souvenirs, you can find most of the same merchandise elsewhere. Try to minimize the time you spend on carnival-type rides; you've probably got an amusement park, carnival, or state fair closer to your hometown. (Don't, however, mistake rides like Space Mountain and the Big Thunder Mountain Railroad as being amusement park rides. They may be of the roller coaster genre, but they represent pure Disney genius.) Similarly, do not devote a lot of time to waiting in lines for meals. Food at most Magic Kingdom eateries is mediocre and uninspiring at best. Eat a good early breakfast before you come and snack on vendor-sold foods during the touring day.

Main Street, U.S.A.

Main Street opens a half-hour to an hour before, and closes a half-hour to an hour after, the rest of the park. This section of the Magic Kingdom is where you'll begin and end your visit. We have already mentioned that assistance and information are available at City Hall. The Walt Disney World Railroad stops at the Main Street Station: you can board here for a grand-circle tour of the Magic Kingdom, or you can get off the train in Frontierland or Mickey's Birthdayland.

Main Street is a replication of a turn-of-the-century American small town street. Many visitors are surprised to discover that all the buildings are real as opposed to being elaborate props. Attention to detail here is exceptional with interiors, furnishings, and fixtures conforming to the period. As with any real Main Street the Disney version is essentially a collection of shops and eating places, with a city hall, a fire station, an old-time cinema, and an attraction detailing the life of Walt Disney, *Walt Disney Story*, thrown in for good measure. Horsedrawn trolleys, double-decker buses, fire engines, and horseless carriages offer rides along Main Street and transport visitors to the central hub.

—— Main Street Services ——

Most of the park's service facilities are centered in the Main Street section, including the following:

Wheelchair & Stroller Rental	To the right of the main entrance before passing under the Railroad Station
Banking Services/ Currency Exchange	To the left of City Hall at the Railroad Station end of Main Street
Storage Lockers	On the ground floor of the Railroad Station at the end of Main Street
Lost & Found	City Hall Building at the Railroad Station end of Main Street

Live Entertainment and Parade Information	City Hall Building at the Railroad Station end of Main Street
Lost Persons	City Hall Building
Diamond Horseshoe Jamboree Reservations	Hospitality House, next to *Walt Disney Story*
Walt Disney World & Local Attraction Information	City Hall Building
First Aid	Next to the Crystal Palace around the central hub to the left (towards Adventureland)
Baby Center/Baby Care Needs	Next to the Crystal Palace around the central hub to the left (towards Adventureland)

—— *Main Street Attractions* ——

Walt Disney World Railroad

Type of Attraction: Scenic railroad ride around the perimeter of the Magic Kingdom. Also transportation to Frontierland and Mickey's Birthdayland.

When to Go: After 11 A.M. or when you need transportation

Special Comments: Main Street is usually the least congested station.

Authors' Rating: Plenty to see; ★★★½ [Critical ratings are based on a scale of zero to five stars. Five stars is the best possible rating.]

Overall Appeal by Age Group:

Pre- school	Grade School	Teens	Young Adults	Over 30	Senior Citizens
★★★★	★★★★	★★½	★★★	★★★½	★★★½

Duration of Ride: About 19 minutes for a complete circuit

Average Wait in Line per 100 People Ahead of You: 8 minutes

Assumes: 2 or more trains operating

Loading Speed: Fast

DESCRIPTION AND COMMENTS   A transportation ride that blends an unusual variety of sights and experiences with an energy-saving way of getting around the park. The train provides a glimpse of all the lands except Adventureland.

TOURING TIPS   Save the train ride until after you have seen the featured attractions, or use when you need transportation. On busy days, lines form at the Frontierland Station, but rarely at the Main Street and Mickey's Birthdayland Stations.

The Walt Disney Story

Type of Attraction: Nostalgic look at the Disney success story
When to Go: During the hot, crowded period of the day
Authors' Rating: A happy remembrance; ★★★★
Overall Appeal by Age Group:

Pre-school	Grade School	Teens	Young Adults	Over 30	Senior Citizens
★★½	★★★	★★★	★★★½	★★★★½	★★★★½

Duration of Presentation: 23 minutes
Pre-Show Entertainment: Disney exhibits
Probable Waiting Time: Less than 10 minutes

DESCRIPTION AND COMMENTS   A warm and well-produced remembrance of the man who started it all. Well worth seeing, especially touching for those old enough to remember Walt Disney.

TOURING TIPS   You usually do not have to wait long for this show, so see it during the busy times of the day when lines are long elsewhere or as you are leaving the park.

Main Street Cinema

Type of Attraction: Old-time movies and vintage Disney cartoons
When to Go: Whenever you want
Authors' Rating: Wonderful selection of hilarious flicks; ★★★½
Overall Appeal by Age Group:

Pre-school	Grade School	Teens	Young Adults	Over 30	Senior Citizens
★★½	★★★	★★★	★★★½	★★★½	★★★½

Duration of Presentation: Runs continuously
Pre-Show Entertainment: None
Probable Waiting Time: No waiting

DESCRIPTION AND COMMENTS   Excellent old-time movies including some vintage Disney cartoons. Since the movies are silent, six are shown simultaneously. No seats; viewers stand.

TOURING TIPS   Good place to get out of the sun or rain, or to kill time while others in your group shop on Main Street. Not something you can't afford to miss.

—— *Main Street Minor Attractions* ——

Transportation Rides

DESCRIPTION AND COMMENTS   Trolleys, buses, etc., which add color to Main Street.

TOURING TIPS   Will save you a walk to the central hub. Not worth waiting in line.

Penny Arcade

DESCRIPTION AND COMMENTS   The Penny Arcade features some vintage arcade machines which can actually be played for a penny or a nickel. Located toward the central hub end of Main Street on the left as you face the Castle.

TOURING TIPS   If you arrive early when Main Street is the only part of the park open, you might want to spend a few minutes here.

Main Street Restaurants and Shops

DESCRIPTION AND COMMENTS   Some of the Magic Kingdom's better food and specialty/souvenir shopping in a nostalgic, happy setting.

Incidentally, the Emporium on Main Street and Mickey's Mart in Tomorrowland are the two best places for finding Disney trademark souvenirs.

TOURING TIPS   The shops are fun but the merchandise can be had elsewhere (except for certain Disney trademark souvenirs). If seeing the park attractions is your objective, save the Main Street eateries and shops until the end of the day. If shopping is your objective, you will find the shops most crowded during the noon hour and near closing time. Remember, Main Street opens at least a half hour earlier, and closes a half hour to an hour later than the rest of Walt Disney World.

The Crystal Palace, at the central hub end of Main Street (towards Adventureland) provides good cafeteria service and is often overlooked by the lunch-hour (but not dinner-hour) masses. Give it a try if you are nearby at the noon hour.

Adventureland

Adventureland is the first land to the left of Main Street and combines a safari/African motif with an old New Orleans/Caribbean motif.

Swiss Family Treehouse

Type of Attraction: Walk-through exhibit

When to Go: Before 11:30 A.M. and after 5 P.M.

Special Comments: Requires climbing a lot of stairs

Authors' Rating: A very creative exhibit; ★★★★

Overall Appeal by Age Group:

Pre-school	Grade School	Teens	Young Adults	Over 30	Senior Citizens
★★★★	★★★★	★★★★	★★★★	★★★★	★★★★

Duration of Tour: 10–15 minutes

Average Wait in Line per 100 People Ahead of You: 7 minutes

Assumes: Normal staffing

Loading Speed: Does not apply

DESCRIPTION AND COMMENTS A fantastic replication of the ship-wrecked family's home will fire the imagination of the inventive and the adventurous.

TOURING TIPS A self-guided walk-through tour which involves a lot of climbing up and down stairs, but no ropes or ladders or anything fancy. People stopping during the walk-through to look extra long or to rest sometimes create bottlenecks which slow crowd flow. We recommend visiting this attraction in the late afternoon or early evening if you are on a one-day tour schedule, or first thing in the morning of your second day.

Jungle Cruise

Type of Ride: A Disney boat ride adventure

When to Go: Before 11 A.M. or two hours before closing

Authors' Rating: A long-enduring Disney masterpiece; ★★★★

Overall Appeal by Age Group:

Pre-school	Grade School	Teens	Young Adults	Over 30	Senior Citizens
★★★★★	★★★★★	★★★★	★★★★½	★★★★½	★★★★½

Duration of Ride: 8–9 minutes

Average Wait in Line per 100 People Ahead of You: 3½ minutes

Assumes: 10 boats operating

Loading Speed: Moderate to fast

DESCRIPTION AND COMMENTS   A boat ride through jungle waterways. Passengers encounter elephants, lions, hostile natives, and a menacing hippo. A long-enduring Disney favorite, with the boatman's spiel adding measurably to the fun.

TOURING TIPS   One of the park's "not to be missed" attractions. Good staffing and an improved management plan have speeded up the lines for this ride.

Pirates of the Caribbean

Type of Ride: A Disney adventure boat ride

When to Go: Between 11:30 A.M. and 4:30 P.M.

Special Comments: This ride frightens some small children.

Authors' Rating: Our pick as the best attraction at Walt Disney World; ★★★★★

Overall Appeal by Age Group:

Pre-school	Grade School	Teens	Young Adults	Over 30	Senior Citizens
★★★	★★★★★	★★★★★	★★★★★	★★★★★	★★★★★

Duration of Ride: Approximately 7½ minutes

Average Wait in Line per 100 People Ahead of You: 1½ minutes

Assumes: Both waiting lines operating

Loading Speed: Fast

DESCRIPTION AND COMMENTS   Another boat ride, this time indoors, through a series of sets depicting a pirate raid on an island settlement, from the bombardment of the fortress to the debauchery that follows the victory. All in good, clean fun.

TOURING TIPS   Another "not to be missed" attraction. Undoubtedly one of the most elaborate and imaginative attractions in the Magic Kingdom. Engineered to move large crowds in a hurry, Pirates is a good attraction to see during the busy middle part of the day. It has two waiting lines, both under cover (try the one on the left).

Tropical Serenade (Enchanted Tiki Birds)

Type of Attraction: AudioAnimatronic Pacific Island musical show
When to Go: Before 11 A.M. and after 3:30 P.M.
Authors' Rating: Very, very unusual; ★★★½
Overall Appeal by Age Group:

Pre-school	Grade School	Teens	Young Adults	Over 30	Senior Citizens
★★½	★★★	★★	★★★½	★★★½	★★★½

Duration of Presentation: 15½ minutes
Pre-Show Entertainment: Talking birds
Probable Waiting Time: 15 minutes

DESCRIPTION AND COMMENTS   An unusual sit-down theater performance where more than two hundred birds, flowers, and Tiki-god statues sing and whistle through a musical program.

TOURING TIPS   One of the more bizarre of the Magic Kingdom's entertainments, but usually not too crowded. We like it in the late afternoon when we can especially appreciate sitting for a bit in an airconditioned theater.

Adventureland Eateries and Shops

DESCRIPTION AND COMMENTS   More specialty shopping a la Banana Republic; and several restaurants, which tend to be less crowded during lunch.

TOURING TIPS   The Adventureland Veranda Restaurant is a good bet for less congestion and speedier service between 11:30 A.M. and 1:30 P.M. Give it a try if you are in the area during lunchtime.

Frontierland

Frontierland adjoins Adventureland as you move clockwise around the Magic Kingdom. The focus here is on the Old West with stockade-type structures and pioneer trappings.

Big Thunder Mountain Railroad

Type of Ride: Tame roller coaster with exciting special effects

When to Go: Before 11 A.M. or after 5:30 P.M.

Special Comments: Children must be 3'4" tall to ride. Those under 7 years must ride with an adult.

Authors' Rating: Great effects/relatively tame ride; ★★★★

Overall Appeal by Age Group:

Pre-school	Grade School	Teens	Young Adults	Over 30	Senior Citizens
★★★	★★★★	★★★★	★★★★	★★★★	★★★★

Duration of Ride: Almost 3½ minutes

Average Wait in Line per 100 People Ahead of You: 2½ minutes

Assumes: Both tracks and 5 trains operating

Loading Speed: Moderate to fast

DESCRIPTION AND COMMENTS A roller coaster ride through and around a Disney "mountain." The time is Gold Rush days, and the idea is that you are on a runaway mine train. Along with the usual thrills of a roller coaster ride (about a 5 on a "scary scale" of 10), the ride showcases some first-rate examples of Disney creativity; lifelike scenes depicting a mining town, falling rocks, and an earthquake, all humorously animated.

TOURING TIPS A superb Disney experience, but not too wild of a roller coaster. The emphasis here is much more on the sights than on the thrill of the ride itself. Regardless, it's a "not to be missed" attraction. The best bet for riding Big Thunder without a long wait in line is to ride early in the morning or between 10:00–11:00 when the ride has been brought up to peak carrying capacity.

Diamond Horseshoe Jamboree

Type of Attraction: Live song/dance/comedy stage show

When to Go: As per your reservations

Special Comments: Seating by reservation only, made on the day of the show, at the Hospitality House on Main Street. No reservations taken at the Saloon itself. Lunch is available.

Authors' Rating: Absolutely superb, not to be missed; ★★★★★

Overall Appeal By Age Group:

Pre-school	Grade School	Teens	Young Adults	Over 30	Senior Citizens
★★★½	★★★★	★★★★	★★★★★	★★★★★	★★★★★

Duration of Presentation: About 30 minutes

Pre-Show Entertainment: 5 minutes

Probable Waiting Time: See Touring Tips

DESCRIPTION AND COMMENTS   A half-hour, G-rated re-creation of an Old West dance hall show, with dancing, singing, and lots of corny comedy. Visitors are seated at tables where snacks and beverages (non-alcoholic) can be ordered before the show. This is a clever, wonderfully cast, uproariously funny show that you should try to work into your schedule.

TOURING TIPS   Though an excellent show (ranked as "not to be missed" for the first time in this edition), it is a real hassle to see, particularly if you have only one day at the Magic Kingdom. Here's why: Seating is by reservation only, made in person on the day you want to see the show. To obtain a reservation you have to go to the Hospitality House on Main Street. Reservation lines move very slowly because every visitor needs to ask questions and receive instructions. If you are able to obtain a reservation for one of the several shows you will be required to appear for seating one-half hour before showtime when you will wait in line again (this time to be admitted to the theater). Once allowed inside you will wait for another fifteen minutes for food orders to be taken and processed before the show finally begins. By observation and experimentation we have determined that a Magic Kingdom visitor spends an average of 20 minutes making his reservation, and forty-five minutes waiting for the show to begin, plus changing his other touring plans to get back to Frontierland in time to be seated. Thus, counting the show itself: a 1½-hour investment of valuable time to see a thirty-minute song-and-dance show. We recommend that you see the Jamboree on your second day, if you have one. For those with only one day, we have incorporated the Diamond Horseshoe into our One-Day Touring Plans as an option that combines the show with lunch and eliminates as much wasted time as possible. See "Magic Kingdom One-Day Touring Plans," pages 114–30.

Country Bear Jamboree

Type of Attraction: AudioAnimatronic country hoedown stage show
When to Go: Before noon and during the 2 hours before closing
Special Comments: Changes shows at Christmas and during the summer
Authors' Rating: A Disney classic, not to be missed; ★★★★½
Overall Appeal by Age Group:

Pre-school	Grade School	Teens	Young Adults	Over 30	Senior Citizens
★★★★	★★★★	★★★★	★★★★½	★★★★½	★★★★½

Duration of Presentation: 15 minutes
Pre-Show Entertainment: None
Probable Waiting Time: This is a very popular attraction with a comparatively small seating capacity. An average waiting time on a busy day between the hours of noon and 5:30 P.M. would be from 30 to 50 minutes.

DESCRIPTION AND COMMENTS   A cast of charming AudioAnimatronic (robotic) bears sing and stomp their way through a Western-style hoedown. One of the Magic Kingdom's most humorous and upbeat shows.

TOURING TIPS   Yet another "not to be missed" attraction, the Jamboree is extremely popular and draws large crowds even early in the day. We recommend seeing this one before 11:30 A.M.

Tom Sawyer Island and Fort Sam Clemens

Type of Attraction: Walk-through exhibit/rustic playground
When to Go: Mid-morning through late afternoon

Special Comments: Closes at dusk
Authors' Rating: The place for rambunctious kids; ★★★★
Overall Appeal by Age Group:

Pre-school	Grade School	Teens	Young Adults	Over 30	Senior Citizens
★★★★★	★★★★★	★★★½	★★★	★★★	★★★

DESCRIPTION AND COMMENTS   Tom Sawyer Island manages to impart something of a sense of isolation from the rest of the park. It has hills to climb, a cave and a windmill to explore, a tipsy barrel bridge to cross, and paths to follow. It's a delight for adults and a godsend for children who have been in tow all day. They love the freedom of the exploration and the excitement of firing air guns from the walls of Ft. Sam Clemens. There's even a "secret" escape tunnel.

TOURING TIPS   Tom Sawyer Island is not one of the Magic Kingdom's more celebrated attractions, but it's certainly one of the better done. Attention to detail is excellent and kids particularly revel in its adventuresome frontier atmosphere. We think it's a must for families with children five through fifteen. If your party is adult, visit the island on your second day or stop by on your first day if you have seen the attractions you most wanted to see.

We like Tom Sawyer Island from about noon until the island closes at dusk. Access is by raft from Frontierland and you will have to stand in line to board both coming and going. Two rafts operate simultaneously, however, and the round trip is usually pretty efficient. Tom Sawyer Island takes about forty-five minutes or so to see; many children could spend a whole day visiting.

Davy Crockett's Explorer Canoes

Type of Ride: Scenic canoe ride
When to Go: Before noon or after 5 P.M.
Special Comments: Skip if the lines are long. Closes at dusk
Authors' Rating: The most fun way of seeing the Rivers of America; ★★★★
Overall Appeal by Age Group:

Pre-school	Grade School	Teens	Young Adults	Over 30	Senior Citizens
★★★★	★★★★	★★★★	★★★★	★★★★	★★★★

Duration of Ride: 9–15 minutes depending how fast you paddle
Average Wait in Line per 100 People Ahead of You: 28 minutes
Assumes: 3 canoes operating
Loading Speed: Slow

DESCRIPTION AND COMMENTS   Paddle-powered ride (your power) around Tom Sawyer Island and Ft. Sam Clemens. Runs the same route with the same sights as the Liberty Square Riverboat and the Mike Fink Keelboats. The canoes only operate during the busy times of the year. The sights are fun and the ride is a little different in that the tourists paddle the canoe.

TOURING TIPS   The canoes represent one of three ways to see the same territory. Since the canoes and keelboats are slower loading, we usually opt for the large riverboat. If you are not up for a boat ride, a different view of the same sights can be had hoofing around Tom Sawyer Island and Ft. Sam Clemens.

Frontierland Shootin' Gallery

Type of Attraction: Electronic shooting gallery
When to Go: Whenever convenient
Special Comments: Costs 25 cents per play
Authors' Rating: A very nifty shooting gallery; ★★★½
Overall Appeal by Age Group:

Pre-school	Grade School	Teens	Young Adults	Over 30	Senior Citizens
★★★½	★★★½	★★★½	★★★½	★★★½	★★★½

DESCRIPTION AND COMMENTS   A very elaborate shooting gallery, this is one of the few attractions not included in the Magic Kingdom admission.

TOURING TIPS   Good fun for them "what likes to shoot," but definitely not a place to be blowing your time if you are on a tight schedule. Try it on your second day if time allows.

Walt Disney World Railroad

DESCRIPTION AND COMMENTS   The Walt Disney World Railroad stops in Frontierland on its circle-tour around the park. See the description of the Walt Disney World Railroad under Main Street for additional detail regarding the sights enroute.

TOURING TIPS   A pleasant and feet-saving way to commute to Main Street and Mickey's Birthdayland. Be advised, however, that the Frontierland Station is usually more congested than its two counterparts.

Frontierland Eateries and Shops

DESCRIPTION AND COMMENTS   Coonskin caps and western-theme specialty shopping, along with fast food eateries that are usually very crowded between 11:30 A.M. and 2 P.M.

TOURING TIPS   Don't waste time browsing shops or standing in line for food unless you have a very relaxed schedule or came specifically to shop.

Liberty Square

Liberty Square recreates the atmosphere of Colonial America at the time of the American Revolution. Architecture is Federal or Colonial, with a real 130-year-old live oak (dubbed the "Liberty Tree") lending dignity and grace to the setting.

Hall of Presidents

Type of Show: AudioAnimatronic historical presentation

When to Go: Before noon or after 4 P.M.

Authors' Rating: Impressive and moving; ★★★★

Overall Appeal by Age Group:

Pre-school	Grade School	Teens	Young Adults	Over 30	Senior Citizens
★	★★★	★★★	★★★½	★★★★	★★★★

Duration of Presentation: Almost 23 minutes

Pre-Show Entertainment: None

Probable Waiting Time: Lines for this attraction LOOK awesome but are usually swallowed up as the theater turns over. If you go during the times suggested above, your wait will probably be the remaining time of the show that's in progress when you arrive. Even during the busiest times of the day, however, waits rarely exceed 40 minutes.

DESCRIPTION AND COMMENTS   A twenty-minute strongly inspirational and patriotic program highlighting milestones in American history. The performance climaxes with a roll call of presidents from Washington through the present, with a few words of encouragement from President Lincoln. A very moving show coupled with one of Disney's best and most ambitious AudioAnimatronics (robotic) efforts.

TOURING TIPS   Definitely a "not to be missed" attraction. The detail and costume of the chief executives is incredible, and if your children tend to fidget during the show, take notice of the fact that the Presidents do, too. This attraction is one of the most popular, particularly among older visitors, and draws large crowds from 11 A.M. through about 5 P.M. Do not be dismayed by the lines, however. The theater holds more than 700 people, thus swallowing up large lines at a single gulp when visitors are admitted. One show is always in progress while the lobby is being filled for the next show. At less than busy times you will probably be admitted directly to the lobby without waiting in line. When the waiting lobby fills, those remaining in line outside are held in place until those in the lobby move into the theater just prior to the next show, at which time another 700 people from the outside line are admitted to the lobby.

Liberty Square Riverboat

Type of Ride: Scenic boat ride
When to Go: Before 12:30 P.M. or after 3:30 P.M.
Authors' Rating: Provides an excellent vantage point; ★★★
Overall Appeal by Age Group:

Pre- school	Grade School	Teens	Young Adults	Over 30	Senior Citizens
★★★	★★★	★★½	★★★	★★★	★★★

Duration of Ride: About 16 minutes
Average Wait to Board: 10–14 minutes
Assumes: Normal operations

DESCRIPTION AND COMMENTS   Large-capacity paddle wheel riverboat that navigates the waters around Tom Sawyer Island and Ft. Sam Clemens. A beautiful craft, the riverboat provides a lofty perspective of Frontierland and Liberty Square.

TOURING TIPS   One of three boat rides that survey the same real estate. Since Davy Crockett's Explorer Canoes and the Mike Fink Keelboats are slower loading, we think the riverboat is the best bet. If you are not in the mood for a boat ride, much of the same sights can be seen by hiking around the island.

Haunted Mansion

Type of Ride: A Disney one-of-its-kind
When to Go: Before 11:30 A.M. or after 3:30 P.M.

Special Comments: This ride does frighten some very small children.

Authors' Rating: Some of Walt Disney World's best special
effects; ★★★★★

Overall Appeal by Age Group:

Pre-school	Grade School	Teens	Young Adults	Over 30	Senior Citizens
Varies	★★★★★	★★★★½	★★★★½	★★★★½	★★★★½

Duration of Ride: 7-minute ride plus a 1½-minute pre-show

Average Wait in Line per 100 People Ahead of You: 2½ minutes

Assumes: Both "stretch rooms" operating

Loading Speed: Fast

DESCRIPTION AND COMMENTS   A fun attraction more than a scary one
with some of the best special effects in the Magic Kingdom. In their
guidebook the Disney people say, "Come face to face with 999 happy
ghosts, ghouls, and goblins in a 'frightfully funny' adventure." That
pretty well sums it up. Be warned that some youngsters become overly
anxious concerning what they think they will see. The actual attraction
scares almost nobody.

TOURING TIPS   This attraction would be more at home in Fantasyland,
but no matter, it's Disney at its best; another "not to be missed" feature.
Lines at the Haunted Mansion ebb and flow more than do the lines of
most other Magic Kingdom high spots. This is due to the Mansion's
proximity to the *Hall of Presidents* and the Liberty Square Riverboat.
These two attractions disgorge 750 and 450 people respectively at one
time every time they turn over. Many of these folks head right over and
hop in line at the Haunted Mansion. Try this attraction before noon and
after 4:30 P.M. and make an effort to slip in between crowds.

Mike Fink Keelboats

Type of Ride: Scenic boat ride

When to Go: Before 11:30 A.M. or after 5 P.M.

Special Comments: Don't ride if the lines are long. Closes at dusk

Authors' Rating: ★★★

Overall Appeal by Age Group:

Pre-school	Grade School	Teens	Young Adults	Over 30	Senior Citizens
★★★½	★★★	★★★	★★★	★★★	★★★

Duration of Ride: 9½ minutes
Average Wait in Line per 100 People Ahead of You: 15 minutes
Assumes: 2 boats operating
Loading Speed: Slow

DESCRIPTION AND COMMENTS   Small river keelboats which circle Tom Sawyer Island and Ft. Sam Clemens, taking the same route as Davy Crockett's Explorer Canoes and the Liberty Square Riverboat. The top deck of the keelboat is exposed to the elements.

TOURING TIPS   This trip covers the same circle traveled by Davy Crockett's Explorer Canoes and the Liberty Square Riverboat. Since the keelboats and the canoes load slowly we prefer the riverboat. Another way to see much of the area covered by the respective boat tours is to explore Tom Sawyer Island and Ft. Sam Clemens on foot.

Liberty Square Eateries and Shops

DESCRIPTION AND COMMENTS   American crafts and souvenir shopping, along with one restaurant, the Liberty Tree Tavern, which is often overlooked by the crowds at lunch.

TOURING TIPS   If you feel like relaxing over a full-service meal, try the Liberty Tree Tavern.

Fantasyland

Truly an enchanting place, spread gracefully like a miniature Alpine village beneath the lofty towers of Cinderella Castle, Fantasyland is the heart of the Magic Kingdom.

It's a Small World

Type of Ride: Scenic boat ride

When to Go: Between 11 A.M. and 5 P.M.

Authors' Rating: A delightful change of pace; ★★★★

Overall Appeal by Age Group:

Pre-school	Grade School	Teens	Young Adults	Over 30	Senior Citizens
★★★★	★★★½	★★★	★★★★	★★★★	★★★★

Duration of Ride: Approximately 11 minutes

Average Wait in Line per 100 People Ahead of You: 1¾ minutes

Assumes: Busy conditions with 30 or more boats operating

Loading Speed: Fast

DESCRIPTION AND COMMENTS   A happy, upbeat attraction with a world brotherhood theme and a catchy tune that will roll around in your head for weeks. Small boats convey visitors on a tour around the world, with singing and dancing dolls showcasing the dress and culture of each nation. Almost everyone enjoys It's a Small World, but it stands, along with the *Enchanted Tiki Birds*, as an attraction that some could take or leave while others think it is one of the real masterpieces of the Magic Kingdom. We rank it as a "not to be missed" attraction. Try it and form your own opinion.

TOURING TIPS   A "not to be missed" attraction, It's a Small World is a fast-loading ride with two waiting lines—try the line on the left. Usually a good bet during the busier times of the day.

Skyway to Tomorrowland

Type of Ride: Scenic transportation to Fantasyland

When to Go: Before noon or during special events

Special Comments: If there is a line it will probably be quicker to walk.

Authors' Rating: Nice view; ★★★½

Overall Appeal by Age Group:

Pre-school	Grade School	Teens	Young Adults	Over 30	Senior Citizens
★★★★	★★★★	★★★½	★★★½	★★★½	★★★½

Duration of Ride: Approximately 5 minutes one way

Average Wait in Line per 100 People Ahead of You: 10 minutes

Assumes: 45 or more cars operating

Loading Speed: Moderate

DESCRIPTION AND COMMENTS   Part of the Magic Kingdom internal transportation system, the Skyway is a chairlift that conveys tourists high above the park to Tomorrowland. The view is great, and sometimes the Skyway can even save a little shoe leather. Usually, however, you could arrive in Tomorrowland much faster by walking.

TOURING TIPS   We enjoy this scenic trip in the morning, during the afternoon Character Parade, during an evening Electrical Parade, or just before closing (this ride opens later and closes earlier than other rides in Fantasyland). In short, before the crowds fill the park, when they are otherwise occupied or when they are on the decline. These times also provide the most dramatic and beautiful vistas.

Peter Pan's Flight

Type of Ride: A Disney fantasy adventure

When to Go: Before 11:30 A.M. or after 5 P.M.

Authors' Rating: Happy, mellow and well done; ★★★★

Overall Appeal by Age Group:

Pre-school	Grade School	Teens	Young Adults	Over 30	Senior Citizens
★★★★	★★★★	★★★½	★★★★	★★★★	★★★★

Duration of Ride: A little over 3 minutes

Average Wait in Line per 100 People Ahead of You: 5½ minutes
Assumes: Normal operation
Loading Speed: Moderate

DESCRIPTION AND COMMENTS   Though not considered to be one of the major attractions, Peter Pan's Flight is superbly designed and absolutely delightful with a happy theme, a reunion with some unforgettable Disney characters, beautiful effects, and charming music.

TOURING TIPS   Though not a major feature of the Magic Kingdom, we nevertheless classify it as "not to be missed." Try to ride before 11:30 A.M. or after 5 P.M., or during the afternoon Character Parade.

Magic Journeys

Type of Show: 3-D fantasy film
When to Go: Between noon and 4 P.M.
Special Comments: Some small children are frightened by the film.
Authors' Rating: Solid production; ★★★★
Overall Appeal by Age Group:

Pre-school	Grade School	Teens	Young Adults	Over 30	Senior Citizens
★★★★	★★★★	★★★½	★★★★	★★★★	★★★★

Duration of Presentation: Approximately 17 minutes
Pre-Show Entertainment: None
Probable Waiting Time: 12 minutes

DESCRIPTION AND COMMENTS   This delightful film was exported to Fantasyland from EPCOT Center when *Captain EO* arrived. A long-time favorite, *Magic Journeys* appeals to all ages. The production is solid, the theme happy and upbeat, and the 3-D effects incredible. All over the theater, children (and many adults) reach out involuntarily to grab objects which seem to be floating out from the screen. The story is about a group of children and their flights of imagination.

TOURING TIPS   We recommend seeing this film during the heat of the day when twenty minutes of relaxing in an air-conditioned theater might improve your attitude. There is almost never a line for this fine attraction.

Cinderella's Golden Carrousel

Type of Ride: Merry-go-round
When to Go: Before 11 A.M. or after 5 P.M.
Special Comments: Adults enjoy the beauty and nostalgia of this ride.
Authors' Rating: A beautiful children's ride; ★★★
Overall Appeal by Age Group:

Pre-school	Grade School	Teens	Young Adults	Over 30	Senior Citizens
★★★★	★★½	★	★★½	★★★	★★★

Duration of Ride: Approximately 2 minutes
Average Wait in Line per 100 People Ahead of You: 5 minutes
Assumes: Normal staffing
Loading Speed: Slow

DESCRIPTION AND COMMENTS   A merry-go-round to be sure, but certainly one of the most elaborate and beautiful you will ever see, especially when the lights are on.

TOURING TIPS   Unless there are small children in your party we suggest you appreciate this ride from the sidelines. If your children insist on riding, try to get on before 11 A.M. or after 5 P.M. While nice to look at, the Carrousel loads and unloads very slowly.

Mr. Toad's Wild Ride

Type of Ride: Disney version of a spook-house track ride
When to Go: Before noon or after 5 P.M.
Authors' Rating: Disappointing; ★½
Overall Appeal by Age Group:

Pre-school	Grade School	Teens	Young Adults	Over 30	Senior Citizens
★★★½	★★★	★★	★★	★★	★★

Duration of Ride: About 2¼ minutes
Average Wait in Line per 100 People Ahead of You: 5½ minutes
Assumes: Both tracks operating
Loading Speed: Slow to moderate

DESCRIPTION AND COMMENTS   This is an amusement park spook

house that does not live up to most visitors' expectations or to the Disney reputation for high quality. The facade is intriguing; the size of the building which houses the attraction suggests an elaborate ride. As it happens, the building is cut in half with the same lackluster ride reproduced in both halves. There is, of course, a separate line for each half.

TOURING TIPS   Skip this ride or let the kids ride if you have some extra time and the lines are short. Also, don't worry that the ride is called "wild"; it's not.

Snow White's Scary Adventures

Type of Ride: Disney version of a spook-house track ride
When to Go: Before 11:30 A.M. and after 5 P.M.
Special Comments: Not really very scary
Authors' Rating: Worth seeing if the wait is not long; ★★★
Overall Appeal by Age Group:

Pre-school	Grade School	Teens	Young Adults	Over 30	Senior Citizens
★★★	★★★	★★½	★★★	★★★	★★★

Duration of Ride: Almost 2½ minutes
Average Wait in Line per 100 People Ahead of You: 6¼ minutes
Assumes: Normal operation
Loading Speed: Moderate

DESCRIPTION AND COMMENTS   Here you ride in a mining car through a spook house featuring Snow White as she narrowly escapes harm at the hands of the wicked witch. The action and effects are a cut above Mr. Toad's Wild Ride but not as good as Peter Pan's Flight.

TOURING TIPS   This ride is not great, but it is good. Experience it if the lines are not too long or on a second day visit. Ride before 11:30 A.M. or after 5 P.M. if possible. Also, don't take the "Scary" part too seriously. The witch looks mean but most kids take her in stride.

20,000 Leagues Under the Sea

Type of Ride: Adventure/scenic boat ride
When to Go: Before 10 A.M. or during the hour before the park closes

Authors' Rating: Interesting and fun; ★★★★
Overall Appeal by Age Group:

Pre-school	Grade School	Teens	Young Adults	Over 30	Senior Citizens
★★★★	★★★★	★★★	★★★½	★★★½	★★★★

Duration of Ride: Approximately 8½ minutes
Average Wait in Line per 100 People Ahead of You: 8 minutes
Assumes: 9 submarines operating
Loading Speed: Slow

DESCRIPTION AND COMMENTS   This attraction is based on the Disney movie of the same title. One of several rides that have been successful at both Disneyland (California) and the Magic Kingdom, the ride consists of a submarine voyage which encounters ocean-floor farming, various marine life (robotic), sunken ships, giant squid attacks, and other sights and adventures. An older ride, it struggles to maintain its image along with such marvels as Pirates of the Caribbean or Space Mountain. All things considered, though, it's still a darn nifty experience, and one that we put in our "not to be missed" category.

TOURING TIPS   This ride could be renamed "20,000 Bottlenecks Under the Sun." It is the traffic engineering nightmare of the Magic Kingdom. Even fifteen minutes after opening, there are long lines and 20- to 30-minute waits. The problem is mainly due to the fact that this slow-loading boat ride is brought up to maximum carrying capacity (nine subs) very tardily. Ride operators fall behind almost as soon as the park opens and never seem to clear the backlog. If you are a Space Mountain fan, make 20,000 Leagues your second stop. If you do not want to ride Space Mountain, ride 20,000 Leagues first thing when the park opens.

Dumbo, the Flying Elephant

Type of Ride: Disneyfied midway ride
When to Go: Before 11 A.M. and after 5 P.M.
Authors' Rating: An attractive children's ride; ★★★½
Overall Appeal by Age Group:

Pre-school	Grade School	Teens	Young Adults	Over 30	Senior Citizens
★★★★	★★★	★★	★½	★½	★½

Duration of Ride: 1½ minutes
Average Wait in Line per 100 People Ahead of You: 20 minutes
Assumes: Normal staffing
Loading Speed: Slow

DESCRIPTION AND COMMENTS   A nice, tame, happy children's ride based on the lovable Disney flying elephant, Dumbo. An upgraded rendition of a ride that can be found at state fairs and amusement parks across the country.

TOURING TIPS   This is a slow-loading ride that we recommend you bypass unless you are on a very relaxed touring schedule. If your kids are excited about Dumbo, try to get them on the ride before 11 A.M. or just before the park closes.

Mad Tea Party

Type of Ride: Midway-type spinning ride
When to Go: Before 11:30 A.M. and after 5 P.M.
Special Comments: You can make the tea cups spin faster by turning the wheel in the center of the cup.
Authors' Rating: Fun, but not worth the wait; ★★
Overall Appeal by Age Group:

Pre-school	Grade School	Teens	Young Adults	Over 30	Senior Citizens
★★★★	★★★★	★★★★	★★½	★★	★★

Duration of Ride: 1½ minutes
Average Wait in Line per 100 People Ahead of You: 7½ minutes
Assumes: Normal staffing
Loading Speed: Slow

DESCRIPTION AND COMMENTS   Well done in the Disney style, but still just an amusement-park ride. The Alice in Wonderland Mad Hatter provides the theme and riders whirl around feverishly in big tea cups. A rendition of this ride, sans Disney characters, can be found at every local carnival and fair.

TOURING TIPS   This ride, aside from not being particularly unique, is notoriously slow loading. Skip it on a busy schedule if the kids will let you. Ride in the morning of your second day if your schedule is more relaxed.

Fantasyland Eateries and Shops

DESCRIPTION AND COMMENTS   If you prefer atmosphere with your dining, you can (with reservations) eat in Cinderella Castle at King Stefan's Banquet Hall. Many of the Magic Kingdom visitors we surveyed wanted to know "What is in the castle?" or "Can we go up into the castle?" Well, Virginia, you can't see the whole thing, but if you eat at King Stefan's you can inspect a fair-sized chunk.

Shops here present more specialty and souvenir shopping opportunities.

TOURING TIPS   To eat at King Stefan's in the castle you must have reservations. Go first thing in the morning and get in line at the door of the restaurant in the interior archway of the castle. We do not recommend a meal at King Stefan's if you are on a tight schedule. If you plan to spend two days in the Magic Kingdom and you are curious about the inside of the castle, you might give it a try on your second day. Don't waste time in the shops unless you have a relaxed schedule or unless shopping is a big priority.

Mickey's Birthdayland

Mickey's Birthdayland is the first new "land" to be added to the Magic Kingdom since its opening, and the only land that does not connect to the central hub. Attractions include a live musical stage show featuring the Disney characters, a chance to meet Mickey Mouse, Mickey Mouse's house, a town (Duckburg) of miniature buildings, a petting farm, and a young children's play area.

All in all, as Whoopi Goldberg might say, Mickey's Birthdayland is a strange piece of work. To begin with, it is sandwiched between Fantasyland and Tomorrowland, like an afterthought, on about three acres that were formerly part of the Grand Prix Raceway. It is by far the smallest of the "lands" and seems more like an attraction than a section of the park.

Though you can wander in on a somewhat obscure path from Fantasyland, Mickey's Birthdayland is basically set up to receive guests arriving via the Walt Disney World Railroad. The idea is that you are on your way to a birthday party for Mickey Mouse (who was 60 years old in 1988). The trains and the stations are all decked out in balloons and other festive party trimmings. As you proceed around the perimeter of the Magic Kingdom on the train, you see various Disney animated characters (in the form of one-dimensional painted plywood cutouts) making their way to the party. Some folks can't get enough of the Disney characters, but we thought the plywood cutouts cheapened the experience of riding the train through Frontierland. Plywood Hueys, Deweys, and Louies seemed terribly out of place in the deep forest just past the stately Frontierland Indian village.

Once you arrive at Mickey's Birthdayland (which is located in the town of Duckburg), there is no indication of where or when this much-hyped party takes place. What you see as you leave the train station is a children's play area on your left, and a street of miniature buildings on your right. There is one normally sized house (Mickey's) among the little buildings, with a cluster of what look like circus tents puffing up colorfully behind.

Mickey's Surprise Party

Type of Show: Live musical comedy featuring the Disney characters

When to Go: Between 11 A.M. and 5 P.M.

Special Comments: After the show, guests can go next door to Mickey's Hollywood Theater to meet Mickey in person backstage.

Authors' Rating: Warm, happy, funny and all Disney; ★★★★

Overall Appeal by Age Group:

Pre-school	Grade School	Teens	Young Adults	Over 30	Senior Citizens
★★★★★	★★★★★	★★★½	★★★★	★★★★	★★★★

Duration of Presentation: Approximately 16 minutes

Pre-Show Entertainment: Mickey Mouse cartoons

Probable Waiting Time: About ten minutes

DESCRIPTION AND COMMENTS   Mickey's Surprise Party, the feature attraction of Mickey's Birthdayland, is reached by walking through Mickey's House (which is full of Mickey Mouse and Walt Disney memorabilia), through Mickey's back yard, and into an air-conditioned, pre-show tent where Mickey Mouse cartoons are viewed on TV monitors. During the summer of 1988, most patrons who found their way this far had no idea that there was anything more to see. They watched cartoons for a few minutes and then turned around and walked out. Had they stayed, they would have been treated to a funny, happy, and energetic live stage show featuring the Disney characters. In the show, which lasts about 16 minutes in all, the characters, under Minnie's supervision, prepare for and subsequently throw Mickey a surprise party.

After the party, guests can exit to Mickey's Hollywood Theater (the building next door), where Mickey receives visitors in his dressing room to pose for photographs. This is a nice touch, but as with the party, this business of meeting Mickey in person backstage is never made very clear. For the most part, folks just walk into Mickey's Hollywood Theater and line up, not knowing what the line is for.

TOURING TIPS   There is no problem catching a performance of Mickey's Surprise Party once you know it's there and how to get to it. We recommend seeing the show during the hot, early afternoon hours when a few minutes in a nice, air-conditioned theater is relaxing. If you want to meet Mickey backstage without a lot of waiting, try one of the following:

1. The last part of the live show involves moving to an adjacent theater to see Mickey's giant cake and to sing *Happy Birthday*. Guests stand during this conclusion of the performance. Position yourself near the exit doors to the left of the giant cake. When the show is over and the doors open, leave quickly and enter the first building on your right. By doing so, you will arrive in the line to meet Mickey ahead of the other 700 some-odd people leaving behind you.

2. Enjoy the petting farm or walk around Duckburg for about 15 minutes after exiting the show. Line up to see Mickey just before the show following yours concludes; this is when the line will be shortest.

—— *Other Mickey's Birthdayland Attractions* ——

Grandma Duck's Petting Farm

Type of Attraction: Walk-through petting farm
When to Go: Any time
Special Comments: Animals are real
Authors' Rating: Could use more animals; ★½
Overall Appeal by Age Group:

Pre-school	Grade School	Teens	Young Adults	Over 30	Senior Citizens
★★★	★★★	★½	★½	★½	★½

DESCRIPTION AND COMMENTS   A modest barn and farm with a dozen or so animals. Unlike most petting farms, this one does not let you walk among the animals (goats, pigs, ducks, chickens, calves, etc.). You must pet them when possible through fences. Much of the attraction is along gravel paths, which make walking very difficult.

TOURING TIPS   Visit the animals any time. You will not encounter large crowds here, as a rule.

Small Children's Play Area

DESCRIPTION AND COMMENTS   This area is designed for small children and features slides, tunnels, ladders, and a variety of other creative playground structures. Children enjoy the chance to let off steam while adults enjoy the tour intermission. The big shortcoming is the lack of shade; attending adults must swelter in the hot Florida sun.

TOURING TIPS   If you are on a tight schedule, skip the playground.

Tomorrowland

Tomorrowland is a futuristic mix of rides and experiences that relate to the technological development of man and what life will be like in the years to come. If this sounds a little bit like the EPCOT Center theme, it's because Tomorrowland was very much a breeding ground for the ideas that resulted in EPCOT Center. Yet Tomorrowland and EPCOT Center are very different. Aside from differences in scale, Tomorrowland is more "just for fun." While EPCOT Center educates in its own delightful style, Tomorrowland allows you to hop in and try the future on for size.

Space Mountain

Type of Ride: Roller coaster in the dark

When to Go: First thing when the park opens or during the hour before closing or between 6 and 7 P.M.

Special Comments: Great fun and action, much wilder than Big Thunder Mountain

Authors' Rating: A great roller coaster with excellent special effects; ★★★★★

Overall Appeal by Age Group:

Pre-school	Grade School	Teens	Young Adults	Over 30	Senior Citizens
†	★★★★★	★★★★★	★★★★½	★★★★	†

†Children must be 3' tall to ride. Some preschoolers loved Space Mountain, others were frightened. The sample size of senior citizens who experienced this ride was too small to develop an accurate rating.

Duration of Ride: Almost 3 minutes

Average Wait in Line per 100 People Ahead of You: 2¾ minutes

Assumes: Two tracks with 14 capsules each at 21-second dispatch intervals

Loading Speed: Moderate to fast

DESCRIPTION AND COMMENTS   Space Mountain is a roller coaster in the dark. Totally enclosed in a mammoth futuristic structure, the attraction is a marvel of creativity and engineering. The theme of the ride is a spaceflight through the dark recesses of the galaxy. The effects are superb and the ride is the fastest and wildest in the Disney repertoire. As a roller coaster, Space Mountain is a lulu, much zippier than the Big Thunder Mountain ride.

TOURING TIPS   Space Mountain is a "not to be missed" feature (if you can handle a fairly wild roller coaster ride). People who are not timid about going on roller coasters will take Space Mountain in stride. What sets Space Mountain apart is that the cars plummet through the dark with only occasional lighting effects piercing the gloom.

Space Mountain is the favorite attraction of many Magic Kingdom visitors between seven and fifty years of age. Each morning prior to opening, particularly during the summer and holiday periods, several hundred S.M. "junkies" crowd the rope barriers at the central hub awaiting the signal to sprint (literally) the 250 yards to the ride's entrance. As our research team called it, the "Space Mountain Morning Mini Marathon" pits tubby, out-of-shape dads and moms against their svelte, speedy offspring, brother against sister, blossoming coeds against truck drivers, nuns against beauticians. If you want to ride Space Mountain without a long wait you had better do well in the "Mini Marathon," because at five minutes after opening, Space Mountain has more guests in line waiting to ride than any five other Magic Kingdom attractions combined.

There was a time when Disney personnel tried to keep guests from running (they still tell you not to run) to Space Mountain, but even in the Magic Kingdom reality is a force to be reckoned with. The reality in this case is that a dozen Disney security personnel cannot control several hundred stampeding, flipped-out, early-morning space cadets. So here you are, a nice normal dental hygienist from Toledo, and you are thinking you'd like to ride Space Mountain. Well Virginia, you're in the big league now; tie up them Reeboks and get ready to run.

But first, a word from the coach. There are a couple of things you can do to get a leg up on the competition. First, arrive early; be one of the first in the park. Proceed to the end of Main Street and cut right past the Plaza Restaurant, and stop under an archway that says:

"The Plaza Pavilion Terrace Dining"

where a Disney worker will be standing behind a rope barrier. From this point, you are approximately 100 yards closer to Space Mountain, on a route through the Plaza Pavilion, than your competition waiting to take off from the central hub. From this point of departure, middle-aged folks walking fast can beat most of the teens sprinting from the central hub. And if you are up to some modest jogging, well . . . . Another advantage of starting from the Plaza Pavilion entrance is that your wait until opening will be cool, comfortable, and in the shade.

If you do not catch Space Mountain early in the morning, try again during the hour before closing. Often at this time of day, Space Mounttain visitors are held in line outside the entrance until all those previously in line have ridden, thus emptying the attraction inside. The appearance from the outside is that the waiting line is enormous when, in reality, the only people waiting are those visible in front of the entrance. This crowd-control technique, known as "stacking," has the effect of discouraging visitors from riding because they perceive the wait to be too long (when in fact the whole line consists only of those standing outside the entrance). Stacking is used in several Walt Disney World rides and attractions during the hour before closing to insure that the ride will be able to close on schedule. For those who do not let the long-appearing line run them off, the waiting period is usually short.

Grand Prix Raceway

Type of Ride: Drive-'em-yourself miniature cars

When to Go: Before 11 A.M. and after 5 P.M.

Special Comments: Must be 4'4" tall to drive

Authors' Rating: Boring; ★

Overall Appeal by Age Group:

Pre-school	Grade School	Teens	Young Adults	Over 30	Senior Citizens
★★★½	★★★	★	½	½	½

Duration of Ride: Approximately 4¼ minutes

Average Wait in Line per 100 People Ahead of You: 4½ minutes

Assumes: 285-car turnover every 20 minutes

Loading Speed: Slow

DESCRIPTION AND COMMENTS   An elaborate miniature raceway with gasoline-powered cars that will travel at speeds of up to seven miles an hour. The raceway design with its sleek cars, racing noises, and Grand Prix billboards is quite alluring. Unfortunately, however, the cars poke along on a track leaving the driver with little to do. Pretty ho-hum for most adults and teenagers. Of those children who would enjoy the ride, many are excluded by the requirement that drivers be 4'4" tall.

TOURING TIPS   This ride is appealing to the eye but definitely expendable to the schedule. Try it your second day if the kids are reluctant to omit it. Ride before 11 A.M. or after 5 P.M.

Skyway to Fantasyland

Type of Ride: Scenic transportation to Fantasyland
When to Go: Before noon and during special events
Special Comments: If there is a line it will probably be quicker to walk.
Authors' Rating: Nice view; ★★★½
Overall Appeal by Age Group:

Pre-school	Grade School	Teens	Young Adults	Over 30	Senior Citizens
★★★★	★★★★	★★★½	★★★½	★★★½	★★★½

Duration of Ride: Approximately 5 minutes one way
Average Wait in Line per 100 People Ahead of You: 10 minutes
Assumes: 45 or more cars operating
Loading Speed: Moderate

DESCRIPTION AND COMMENTS   A skylift that will transport you from Tomorrowland to the far corner of Fantasyland near the border it shares with Liberty Square. The view is one of the best in the Magic Kingdom, but walking is usually faster if you just want to get there.

TOURING TIPS   Unless the lines are short, the Skyway will not save you any time as a mode of transportation. As a ride, however, it affords some incredible views. Ride in the morning, during the two hours before the park closes, or during one of the daily parades (this ride sometimes opens later and closes earlier than other rides in Tomorrowland).

StarJets

Type of Ride: Very mild midway-type thrill ride
When to Go: Before 11 A.M. or after 5 P.M.
Authors' Rating: Not worth the wait; ★

Overall Appeal by Age Group:

Pre-school	Grade School	Teens	Young Adults	Over 30	Senior Citizens
★★★★	★★★½	★★★	★★	★	★

Duration of Ride: 1½ minutes

Average Wait in Line per 100 People Ahead of You: 13½ minutes

Assumes: Normal staffing

Loading Speed: Slow

DESCRIPTION AND COMMENTS   A carnival-type ride involving small rockets which rotate on arms around a central axis.

TOURING TIPS   Slow loading and expendable on any schedule.

WEDway PeopleMover

Type of Ride: Scenic

When to Go: During the hot, crowded period of the day (11:30 A.M.– 4:30 P.M.

Special Comments: A good way to check out the crowd at Space Mountain

Authors' Rating: Scenic, relaxing, informative; ★★★½

Overall Appeal by Age Group:

Pre-school	Grade School	Teens	Young Adults	Over 30	Senior Citizens
★★★	★★★	★★½	★★★	★★★½	★★★½

Duration of Ride: 10 minutes

Average Wait in Line per 100 People Ahead of You: 1½ minutes

Assumes: 39 trains operating

Loading Speed: Fast

DESCRIPTION AND COMMENTS   A unique prototype of a linear induction powered system of mass transportation. Tram-like cars take you on a leisurely tour of Tomorrowland, including a peek at the inside of Space Mountain.

TOURING TIPS   A nice, pleasant, relaxing ride where the lines move quickly and are seldom long. A good ride to take during the busier times of the day.

Carousel of Progress

Type of Show: AudioAnimatronic theater production
When to Go: Between 11:30 A.M. and 4 P.M.
Authors' Rating: Nostalgic, warm and happy; ★★★★½
Overall Appeal by Age Group:

Pre-school	Grade School	Teens	Young Adults	Over 30	Senior Citizens
★★★	★★★½	★★★½	★★★½	★★★★½	★★★★½

Duration of Presentation: 18 minutes
Pre-Show Entertainment: None
Probable Waiting Time: Less than 10 minutes

DESCRIPTION AND COMMENTS   This is a warm and nostalgic look at the way technology and electricity have changed the lives of an Audio-Animatronics family over several generations. Though not rating a "not to be missed" review, General Electric's *Carousel of Progress* is thoroughly delightful. The family depicted is easy to identify with, and a happy, sentimental tune (which you will find yourself humming all day) serves to bridge the gap between generations.

TOURING TIPS   While not on our "not to be missed" list, this attraction is a great favorite of Magic Kingdom repeat visitors. A great favorite of ours as well, it is included on all of our One-Day Touring Plans. *Carousel of Progress* handles big crowds effectively and is a good choice for touring during the busier times of the day.

Dreamflight (opens December 1988)

Type of Ride: Disney educational adventure ride
When to go: Between 11:30 A.M. and 4:30 P.M.
Authors' Rating: Excellent; ★★★★
Projected Overall Appeal by Age Group:

Pre-school	Grade School	Teens	Young Adults	Over 30	Senior Citizens
★★★½	★★★★	★★★★	★★★★	★★★★	★★★★

Duration of Ride: About 4½ minutes
Average Wait in Line per 100 People Ahead of You: 2½ minutes
Assumes: Normal operation

Loading Speed: Fast

DESCRIPTION AND COMMENTS   Presented by Delta Airlines, Dreamflight is a ride-adventure that depicts the history and future of aviation. Both educational and fun, this ride could have fit in very nicely at EPCOT Center.

TOURING TIPS   Dreamflight is an excellent ride that was somewhat lost in the shuffle during all the 1988 and 1989 new additions and grand openings. A fast-loading and high-carrying-capacity ride, Dreamflight is another good choice for midday and late afternoon touring.

World Premier Circle-Vision: American Journeys

Type of Show: Patriotic travelog projected onto multiple screens
When to Go: During the hot, crowded period of the day (11:30 A.M.–4 P.M.)
Special Comments: Audience must stand throughout presentation
Authors' Rating: Wonderful; not to be missed; ★★★★½
Overall Appeal by Age Group:

Pre-school	Grade School	Teens	Young Adults	Over 30	Senior Citizens
★★	★★★½	★★★★	★★★★½	★★★★★	★★★★★

Duration of Presentation: About 20 minutes
Pre-Show Entertainment: About 10 minutes
Probable Waiting Time: Less than 10 minutes

DESCRIPTION AND COMMENTS   Here the visitor stands in the center of a huge theater where multiple projectors make an encircling 360° screen come alive. It's another trip around the world, but this time you not only see where you are going, but what's on either side, and what's behind you. The movie, which demonstrates this cinematic marvel, is fast paced, well produced, and very much deserving of your attention. More than a travelog, *American Journeys* takes you down the awesome rapids of the Colorado River, on a surfing expedition in Hawaii, and in close for a space-shuttle blast-off.

TOURING TIPS   An excellent film and an exciting new motion picture technique make this an attraction you will want to see. The theater has the largest single-room capacity of any theater in the Magic Kingdom, making it a perfect show to see during peak attendance hours.

Mission To Mars

Type of Show: Theater-in-the-round simulation of space journey
When to Go: During the hot, crowded period of the day (11 A.M.–
    4:30 P.M.)
Special Comments: Special effects sometimes frighten toddlers.
Authors' Rating: Worthwhile; ★★★
Overall Appeal by Age Group:

Pre-school	Grade School	Teens	Young Adults	Over 30	Senior Citizens
★★	★★½	★★½	★★★	★★★	★★★

Duration of Presentation: About 12 minutes
Pre-Show Entertainment: About 6 minutes
Probable Waiting Time: Less than 10 minutes

DESCRIPTION AND COMMENTS   Here the visitor takes a simulated space shuttle flight from Earth to Mars. The voyage is both dramatic and educational, with realistic special effects.

TOURING TIPS   A long-enduring Magic Kingdom favorite (formerly Spaceflight to the Moon), this attraction still demands attention. Try to see *Mission to Mars* during the hot crowded period of the day.

Tomorrowland Eateries and Shops

DESCRIPTION AND COMMENTS   The Tomorrowland Terrace is the largest and most efficient of the Magic Kingdom's numerous fast-food restaurants.

Several shops provide yet additional opportunities for buying souvenirs and curiosities.

TOURING TIPS   Forget browsing the shops until your second day unless shopping is your top priority.

Magic Kingdom Ride Information

—— *Cutting Down Your Time in Line
by Understanding the Rides* ——

There are many different types of rides in the Magic Kingdom. Some rides, like Pirates of the Caribbean, are engineered to carry almost 3,500 people every hour. At the other extreme, rides such as Dumbo, the Flying Elephant, can only accommodate around 300 persons in an hour. Most rides fall somewhere in between. Lots of factors figure into how long you will have to wait to experience a particular ride: the popularity of the ride, how it loads and unloads, how many persons can ride at one time, how many units (cars, rockets, boats, flying elephants, Skyway gondolas, etc.) of those available are in service at a given time, and how many staff personnel are available to operate the ride. Let's take them one by one:

1. *How popular is the ride?*

Newer rides like Big Thunder Mountain Railroad attract a lot of people, as do longtime favorites such as 20,000 Leagues Under the Sea. If you know a ride is popular, you need to learn a little more about how it operates to determine when might be the best time to ride. But a ride need not be especially popular to form long lines; the lines can be the result of less than desirable traffic engineering (i.e., it takes so long to load and unload that a line builds up anyway). This is the situation at the Mad Tea Party, Dumbo, the Flying Elephant, and Cinderella's Golden Carrousel. For instance, only a small percentage of the visitors (mostly children) to the Magic Kingdom ride Dumbo, but because it takes so long to load and unload this comparatively less popular ride, long waiting lines form.

2. *How does the ride load and unload?*

Some rides never stop. They are like a circular conveyor belt that goes around and around. We call these "continuous loaders." The Haunted Mansion is a continuous loader, and so are Dreamflight and

Peter Pan's Flight. The number of people that can be moved through in an hour depends on how many cars, pirate ships, or whatever, are on the conveyor. The Haunted Mansion and Dreamflight have lots of cars on the conveyor belt and consequently can move more than 2,500 people an hour. Peter Pan's Flight has fewer cars (or pirate ships in this case) and can handle only about 1,100 people each hour.

Still other rides are "interval loaders." This means that cars are unloaded, loaded, and dispatched at certain set intervals (sometimes controlled manually and sometimes by a computer). Space Mountain is an interval loader. It has two separate tracks (in other words the ride has been duplicated in the same facility). Each track can run up to fourteen space capsules, released at thirty-six-second, twenty-six-second, or twenty-one-second intervals (the bigger the crowd, the shorter the interval). In one kind of interval loader, like Space Mountain, empty cars (space capsules) are returned to the starting point empty where they line up waiting to be reloaded. In a second type of interval loader, one group of riders enters the vehicle while the last group of riders departs. We call these "in and out" interval loaders. It's a Small World is a good example of an in and out interval loader. As a boat pulls up to the dock, those who have just completed their ride exit to the left. At almost the same time, those waiting to ride enter the boat from the right. The boat is released to the dispatch point a few yards down the line where it is launched according to whatever second interval is being used. Interval loaders of both types can be very efficient at moving people if (1) the release (launch) interval is relatively short; and (2) the ride can accommodate a large number of vehicles in the system at one time. Since many boats can be floating through Pirates of the Caribbean at a given time, and since the release interval is short, almost 3,500 people an hour can see this attraction. 20,000 Leagues Under the Sea is an in and out interval loader, but can only run a maximum of nine submarines at a time. Thus 20,000 Leagues can only handle up to 1,800 people an hour.

A third group of rides are "cycle rides." Another name for these same rides is "stop and go" rides. Here those waiting to ride exchange places with those who have just ridden. The main difference between in and out interval rides and cycle rides is that with a cycle ride the whole system shuts down when loading and unloading is in progress. While one boat is loading and unloading in It's a Small World many other boats are advancing through the ride. But when Dumbo, the Flying Elephant, touches down, the whole ride is at a standstill until the next flight is launched. Likewise, with Cinderella's Golden Carrousel, all riders dismount and the Carrousel stands stationary until the next group is mounted and ready to ride. In discussing a cycle ride, the amount of time the ride is in motion is called "ride time." The amount of time that the ride is idle while loading and unloading is called "load time." Load time added to ride time equals "cycle time," or the time expended from the start of one run of the ride until the start of the succeeding run. Cycle rides are the least efficient of all Magic Kingdom rides in terms of traffic engineering.

3. *How many persons can ride at one time?*

This figure is defined in terms of "per-ride capacity" or "system capacity." Either way the figures allude to the number of people who can be riding at the same time. Our discussion above illustrates that the greater the carrying capacity of a ride (all other things being equal) the more visitors it can accommodate in an hour.

4. *How many "units" are in service at a given time?*

A "unit" is simply our term for the vehicle you sit in during your ride. At the Mad Tea Party the unit is a tea cup, at 20,000 Leagues it's a submarine, and at the Grand Prix Raceway it's a race car. On some rides (mostly cycle rides), the number of units in operation at a given time is fixed. Thus, there are always ten flying elephant units operating on the Dumbo ride, ninety horses on Cinderella's Golden Carrousel, and so on. What this fixed number of units means to you is that there is no way to increase the carrying capacity of the ride by adding more units. On a busy day, therefore, the only way to carry more people each hour on a fixed unit cycle ride is to shorten the loading time (which, as we will discuss next, is sometimes impossible) or by decreasing the riding time, the actual time the ride is in motion. The bottom line on a busy day for a cycle ride is that you will wait longer and be rewarded for your wait with a shorter ride. This is why we try to steer you clear of the cycle rides unless you are willing to ride them early in the morning or late at night. The following are cycle rides:

Fantasyland:	Dumbo, the Flying Elephant
	Cinderella's Golden Carrousel
	Mad Tea Party
Tomorrowland:	StarJets

Other rides in the Magic Kingdom can increase their carrying capacity by adding additional units to the system as the crowds build. Big

Thunder Mountain is a good example. If attendance is very light, Big Thunder can start the day by running one of their five available mine trains on one out of two available tracks. If lines start to build the other track can be opened and more mine trains placed into operation. At full capacity a total of five trains on two tracks can carry about 2,400 persons an hour. Likewise Pirates of the Caribbean can increase its capacity by adding more boats, and Snow White's Scary Adventures by adding more mine cars. Sometimes a long line will disappear almost instantly when new units are brought on line. When an interval-loading ride places more units into operation, it usually shortens the dispatch interval, so more units are being dispatched more often.

5. *How many staff personnel are available to operate the ride?*

Allocation of additional staff to a given ride can allow extra units to be placed in operation, or additional loading areas or holding areas to be opened. Pirates of the Caribbean and It's a Small World can run two separate waiting lines and loading zones. The Haunted Mansion has a one-and-a-half-minute preshow which is staged in a "stretch room." On busy days a second stretch room can be activated, thus permitting a more continuous flow of visitors to the actual loading area. Additional staff make a world of difference in some cycle rides. Often, one attendant will operate the Mad Tea Party. This single person must clear the visitors from the ride just completed, admit and seat visitors for the upcoming ride, check that all tea cups are properly secured (which entails an inspection of each tea cup), return to the control panel, issue instructions to the riders, and finally, activate the ride (whew!). A second attendant allows for the division of these responsibilities and has the effect of cutting loading time by 25 to 50 percent.

By knowing the way a ride loads, its approximate hourly capacity, and its relative popularity, we can anticipate which rides are likely to develop long lines, and more importantly, how long we will have to wait to ride.

Magic Kingdom
Theater Information

—— Cutting Down Your Time in Line
by Understanding the Shows ——

Many of the featured attractions in the Magic Kingdom are theater presentations. While not as complex from a traffic engineering viewpoint as rides, a little enlightenment concerning their operation may save some touring time.

Most of the theater attractions in the Magic Kingdom operate in three distinct phases:

1. There are the visitors who are in the theater viewing the presentation.

2. There are the visitors who have passed through the turnstile into a holding area or waiting lobby. These people will be admitted to the theater as soon as the current presentation is concluded. Several attractions offer a preshow in their waiting lobby to entertain the crowd until they are admitted to the main show. Among these are the *Tropical Serenade (Enchanted Tiki Birds)*, and the *Mission to Mars*.

3. There is the outside line. Visitors waiting here will enter the waiting lobby when there is room, and then be moved into the theater when the audience turns over (is exchanged) between shows.

The theater capacity and the popularity of the presentation, along with the level of attendance in the park, determine how long the lines will be at a given theater attraction. Except for holidays and other days of especially heavy attendance, the longest wait for a show should be the time of one complete performance. Expressed differently, when you arrive at a particular show a performance will then be in progress. Under normal circumstances, you have to wait only until that performance ends; at worst, your wait lasts the length of a complete show (if it has just begun).

—— *How to Deal with Obnoxious People* ——

At every theater presentation at both the Magic Kingdom and EPCOT Center, visitors in the preshow area elbow, nudge, and crowd one another in order to make sure that they are admitted to the performance. Not necessary—if you are admitted through the turnstile into the preshow area a seat has automatically been allocated for you in the theater. When it is time to proceed into the theater don't rush; just relax and let other people jam the doorways. When the congestion has been relieved simply stroll in and take a seat.

Attendants at many theaters will instruct you to enter a row of seats and move completely to the far side, filling every seat so that each row can be completely filled. And invariably some inconsiderate, thick-skulled yahoo will plop down right in the middle of the row, stopping traffic or forcing other visitors to climb over him. Take our word for it—there is no such thing as a bad seat. All of the Disney theaters have been designed to provide a near-perfect view from every seat in the house. Our recommendation is to follow instructions and move to the far end of the row, and if you encounter some dummy blocking the middle of the row, have every person in your party step very hard on his toes as you move past him.

The Disney people also ask that visitors not use flash photography in the theaters (the theaters are too dark for the pictures to turn out, *plus* the flash is disruptive to other viewers). Needless to say, this admonition is routinely ignored. Flashers are more difficult to deal with than row-blockers. You can threaten to turn the offenders over to Disney Security, or better yet, simply hold your hand over the lens (you have to be quick) when they raise their cameras.

Live Entertainment in the Magic Kingdom

Live entertainment in the form of bands, Disney character appearances, parades, singing and dancing, and ceremonies further enliven and add color to the Magic Kingdom on a daily basis. For specific information about what's going on the day you visit, stop by City Hall as you enter the park. Be forewarned, however, that if you are on a tight schedule, it is impossible to see both the Magic Kingdom's featured attractions **and** take in the numerous and varied live performances offered. In our One-Day Touring Plans we exclude the live performances in favor of seeing as much of the park as time permits. This is a considered, tactical decision based on the fact that some of the parades and other performances siphon crowds away from the more popular rides, thus shortening waiting lines.

But the color and pageantry of live happenings around the park are an integral part of the Magic Kingdom entertainment mix and a persuasive argument for second-day touring. The following is an incomplete list and description of those performances and events that are scheduled with some regularity and for which no reservations are required.

Spirit of America Singers	A vocal ensemble that sings patriotic and regional classic songs in Liberty Square.
Fantasy Faire Stage	Site of various concerts in Fantasyland
Steel Drum Bands	Steel drum bands perform daily at the Caribbean Plaza in Adventureland.
Frontierland Stuntmen	Stuntmen stage shootouts in Frontierland according to the daily live entertainment schedule.
Kids of the Kingdom	A youthful song and dance group which performs popular music daily in the Castle Forecourt. Disney characters usually join in the fun.

Flag Retreat	Daily at 5:10 P.M. at Liberty Square, a small band and honor guard lower the flag and release a flock of white homing pigeons.
Main Street Parade	A parade down Main Street and around the central hub featuring marching bands, old-time vehicles, floats, and the Disney characters. Check with City Hall for the parade schedule.
The Main Street Electrical Parade	An elaborated version of the Main Street Parade with thirty floats, more than one hundred performers, and "a million twinkling lights," according to Disney spokesmen. The Electrical Parade is performed twice on holidays and on days when the park is open until midnight, usually at 9 P.M. and 11 P.M.
Bay Lake and Seven Seas Lagoon Floating Electrical Pageant	This is one of our favorites of all the Disney extras, but you have to leave the Magic Kingdom to see it. The Floating Electrical Pageant is a stunning electric light show afloat on small barges and set to nifty electronic music. The Pageant is performed at nightfall on the Seven Seas Lagoon and on Bay Lake. Exit the Magic Kingdom and take the monorail to the Contemporary Resort Hotel or to the Polynesian Village. Proceed to get yourself a drink and have a seat at the waterfront; the show will begin shortly.
Fantasy in the Sky	A stellar fireworks display unleashed after dark on those nights the park is open late.
Tomorrowland Terrace Stage	This stage in the Tomorrowland Terrace Restaurant features top-40 rock music.
Disney Character Shows	There are two live Disney character shows. *Mickey's Surprise Party* is the featured attraction of Mickey's Birthdayland and runs continuously. *The Fantasy Follies* performs at the Tomorrowland Theater according to the daily live entertainment schedule.
Magic Kingdom Bands	Various banjo, dixieland, steel drum, marching, and fife and drum bands roam the Magic Kingdom daily.

Walt Disney Character
Appearances

Walt Disney characters appear at random throughout the Magic Kingdom, but with greater frequency in Fantasyland, Mickey's Birthdayland, and on Main Street. Twice each day, according to the live entertainment schedule, characters collect *en masse* in front of Cinderella Castle.

Eating in the Magic Kingdom

The Magic Kingdom is a wonder and a marvel, a testimony to the creative genius of man. But for all of the beauty, imagination, and wholesomeness of this incredible place, it is almost impossible to get a really good meal. Simply put, what is available is that same computerized, homogenized fare that languishes beneath the heat lamps of every fast-food chain restaurant in America. Logistically we are sympathetic; it is overwhelming to contemplate preparing and serving 130,000-or-so meals each day. But our understanding, unfortunately, does not make the food any more palatable. Do not misunderstand, the food at the Magic Kingdom is not awful. It is merely mediocre in a place that has set the standard in virtually every other area for quality in tourism and entertainment. Given the challenge of feeding so many people each day, we might be more accepting of the benign fare if (1) we didn't believe the Disney people could do better, and if (2) obtaining food didn't require such an investment of time and effort. The variety found on the numerous menus indicates that somebody once had the right idea.

—— *Alternatives and Suggestions for Eating in the Magic Kingdom* ——

Remember, this discussion is about the Magic Kingdom. EPCOT Center is a whole new game and is treated separately under a similar heading on page 169.

1. Eat a good breakfast before arriving at the Magic Kingdom. You do not want to waste touring time eating breakfast at the park. Besides, there are some truly outstanding breakfast specials at restaurants outside of Walt Disney World.

2. Having eaten a good breakfast, keep your tummy happy as you tour by purchasing snacks from the many vendors stationed

throughout the Magic Kingdom. This is especially important if you have a tight schedule; you cannot afford to spend a lot of time waiting in line for food.

3. If you are on a tight schedule and the park closes early, stay until closing and eat dinner outside of Walt Disney World before returning to your hotel. If the Magic Kingdom stays open late, eat an early dinner at about 4 P.M. or 4:30 P.M. in the Magic Kingdom eatery of your choice. You should have missed the last wave of lunch diners and sneaked in just ahead of the dinner crowd.

4. If you are on a fairly relaxed schedule with more than one day allocated for touring the Magic Kingdom, try leaving the park for lunch at one of the many restaurants outside of Walt Disney World. The coming and going isn't nearly as time consuming as it appears, and you will probably be able to get a better meal, with faster service, in a more relaxed atmosphere, at a cheaper price.

5. Take the monorail to one of the Theme Resort Hotels for lunch. The trip over and back takes very little time, and because most guests have left the hotels for the parks, the Theme Resort restaurants are often slack. The food is better than in the Magic Kingdom, the service is faster, the atmosphere more relaxed, and beer, wine, and mixed drinks are available. Of the Theme Resorts connected directly to the Magic Kingdom by monorail, we prefer the fare at the Contemporary Resort Hotel. The restaurants at the new Grand Floridian are very good, but pricey.

6. If you decide to eat in the Magic Kingdom during the midday rush (11 A.M.–2 P.M.) or the evening rush (5 P.M.–8 P.M.), try The Crystal Palace towards Adventureland at the central hub end of Main Street, the Adventureland Veranda to the right of the Adventureland entrance bridge, or the Liberty Tree Tavern next to the *Diamond Horseshoe Jamboree*. All three of these eateries serve decent food and usually are not crowded. As another alternative, a lunch-hour reservation for the *Diamond Horseshoe Jamboree* combines a good show with an easy meal.

7. Many of the Magic Kingdom restaurants serve a cold sandwich of one sort or another. It is possible to buy a cold lunch (except

for the drinks) before 11 A.M. and then carry your food until you are ready to eat. We met a family which does this routinely, with Mom always remembering to bring several small plastic bags in which to pack the food. Drinks are purchased at an appropriate time from any convenient drink vendor.

8. Most fast-food eateries in the Magic Kingdom have more than one service window. Regardless of time of day, check out the lines at *all* of the windows before queuing. Sometimes a manned, but out of the way, window will have a much shorter line or no line at all.

9. Restaurants which accept reservations for lunch and/or dinner fill their respective meal seatings quickly. To obtain reservations you must hot-foot it over to the restaurant in question (King Stefan's Banquet Hall, etc.) as soon as you enter the park and blow your most effective touring time waiting in line to make your meal reservation. Often you are asked to return well in advance of your seating time, and even then, on many occasions, you will have to wait well past your scheduled time for your table.

10. For your general information, the Disney people have a park rule against bringing in your own food and drink. We interviewed one woman who, ignoring the rule, brought a huge picnic lunch for her family of five packed into a large diaper/ baby paraphernalia bag. Upon entering the park she secured the bag in a locker under the Main Street Station, to be retrieved later when the family was hungry. A Texas family returned to their camper/truck in the parking lot for lunch where they had a cooler, lawn chairs, and plenty of food a la the college football tailgating tradition.

Shopping in the Magic Kingdom

Shops in the Magic Kingdom add realism and atmosphere to the various theme settings and make available an extensive inventory of souvenirs, clothing, novelties, decorator items, and more. Much of the merchandise displayed (with the exception of Disney trademark souvenir items) is available back home and elsewhere at a lower price. In our opinion, shopping is not one of the main reasons for visiting the Magic Kingdom. We recommend bypassing the shops on a one-day visit. If you have two or more days to spend in the Magic Kingdom, browse the shops during the early afternoon when many of the attractions are crowded. Remember that Main Street, with its multitude of shops, opens one hour earlier and closes one hour later than the rest of the park. Lockers in the Main Street Train Station allow you to stash your purchases safely as opposed to dragging them around the park with you.

Magic Kingdom
One-Day Touring Plans

The Magic Kingdom One-Day Touring Plans are field-tested, step-by-step plans for seeing as much as possible in one day with a minimum of time wasted standing in line. They are designed to assist you in avoiding crowds and bottlenecks on days of moderate to heavy attendance. On days of lighter attendance (see Selecting the Time of Year for Your Visit, page 24), the plans will still save you time, but will not be as critical to successful touring as on busier days. Do not be concerned that other people will be following the same touring strategy, thus rendering it useless. Fewer than 1 of every 300 people in the park will have been exposed to this information.

On days of moderate to heavy attendance follow the One-Day Touring Plan exactly, deviating only:

1. When you do not wish to experience an attraction called for on the Touring Plan. For instance, the Touring Plan may indicate that you go next to Tomorrowland and ride Space Mountain, a roller coaster ride. If you do not enjoy roller coasters, simply skip this step of the plan and proceed to the next step.

2. When you encounter a very long line at an attraction called for by the Touring Plan. Crowds ebb and flow at the Magic Kingdom, and by chance an unusually large line may have gathered at an attraction to which you are directed. For example, upon arrival at the Haunted Mansion, you find the waiting lines to be extremely long. It is possible that this is a temporary situation occasioned by several hundred people arriving en masse from a recently concluded performance of the nearby *Hall of Presidents*. If this is the case, simply skip the Haunted Mansion and move to the next step, returning later in the day to try the Haunted Mansion once again.

Three outline versions of the One-Day Touring Plan follow this section; each is tailored for groups with different needs.

114

—— *Traffic Patterns in the Magic Kingdom* ——

When we began our research on the Magic Kingdom we were very interested in traffic patterns throughout the park, specifically:

1. *Which sections of the park and what attractions do visitors head for when they first arrive?* When visitors are admitted to the various lands during the summer and holiday periods, traffic to Tomorrowland and Fantasyland is heaviest, followed by Adventureland, and then Liberty Square and Mickey's Birthdayland. During the school year when there are fewer young people in the park, early-morning traffic is more evenly distributed, but is still heaviest in Tomorrowland and Fantasyland. In our research we tested the claim, often heard, that most people turn right into Tomorrowland and tour the Magic Kingdom in an orderly counterclockwise fashion. We found it without basis. As the park fills, visitors seem to head for the top attractions, which they wish to ride before the lines get long. This more than any other factor determines traffic patterns in the morning. Attractions which receive considerable patronage in the early morning are:

Tomorrowland:	Space Mountain
Frontierland:	Big Thunder Mountain Railroad
Fantasyland:	20,000 Leagues Under the Sea
Adventureland:	Jungle Cruise

2. *How long does it take for the park to reach peak capacity for a given day? How are the visitors dispersed throughout the park?* Lines sampled reached their longest lengths between noon and 2 P.M., indicating more arrivals than park departures into the early afternoon. For general touring purposes, most attractions developed long lines between 10:30 A.M. and 11:30 A.M. Through the early hours of the morning and the early hours of the afternoon attendance was fairly equally distributed through all of the lands. In late afternoon, however, we noted a concentration of visitors in Fantasyland, Liberty Square, and Frontierland, with a slight decrease of visitors in Adventureland, and a marked decrease of visitors in Tomorrowland. This pattern did not occur consistently day to day, but did happen often enough for us to suggest Tomorrowland as the least crowded land for late afternoon touring.

3. *How do most visitors go about touring the park? Is there a difference in the touring behavior of first-time visitors versus repeat visitors?* Many first-time visitors are accompanied by friends or relatives familiar with the Magic Kingdom, who guide their tour. The tours sometimes do and sometimes do not proceed in an orderly touring sequence. First-time visitors without personal touring guides tend to be more orderly in their touring. Many first-time visitors, however, are drawn to Cinderella Castle upon entering the park and thus commence their rotation from Fantasyland. Repeat visitors usually proceed directly to their favorite attractions.

4. *What effect do special events, such as the daily Main Street Parade, have on traffic patterns?* Special events such as the Main Street Parade do pull substantial numbers of visitors from the ride lines, but the key to the length of the lines remains the number of people in the park.

5. *What are the traffic patterns near to and at closing time?* On our sample days, in season and out of season, park departures outnumbered arrivals beginning mid-afternoon. Many visitors left during the late afternoon as the dinner hour approached. When the park closed early, there were steady departures during the two hours before closing time, with a huge exodus of remaining visitors at closing time. When the park closed late, people left throughout the evening, with departures increasing as closing time approached; a huge throng was still there at closing time. Mass departures at closing time mainly affect conditions on Main Street and at the monorail and ferry stops, due to the crowds generated when the other five lands close. In the other five lands, touring conditions are normally uncrowded just before closing time.

6. *I have heard that when there are two or more lines, the shortest wait is always the left line. Is this true?* We do not recommend the "left-line strategy" because, with the occasional exception of food lines, it simply does not hold up. The Disney people have a number of techniques for both internal and external crowd control which distribute line traffic nearly equally. Placing research team members at the same time in each available line, we could discern no consistent pattern as to who would be served first. Further, staffers entering the same attraction via different lines would almost always exit the attraction within 30 to 90 seconds of each other.

── *Magic Kingdom One-Day Touring Plan, for Adults* ──

FOR: **Adults without small children.**

ASSUMES: Willingness to experience all major rides (including roller coasters) and shows.

DIRECTION	EXPLANATION
1. Arrive at the Transportation and Ticket Center one hour before the park's stated opening time.	This will give you time to park, catch the tram to the ticketing area, buy your admission, and catch the monorail or ferry to the Magic Kingdom.
2. Take the Monorail to the Magic Kingdom from the Transportation and Ticket Center.	Your choice of transportation to the Magic Kingdom consists of a ferryboat or the monorail. Lines are longer for the monorail, but even so, you will usually arrive at the Magic Kingdom ahead of the boat.
3. Having entered the Magic Kingdom, stop briefly at City Hall for a schedule of the day's entertainment offerings while another member of your party hurries to the Hospitality House (across the square from City Hall) to make reservations for the 12:15 P.M. seating of the *Diamond Horseshoe Jamboree*. Rejoin your party at the Hospitality House.	Move quickly here. Pick up your schedule and reservations and move posthaste to the end of Main Street. Since your objective is to beat the crowds to the potential bottlenecks in the other areas of the park, you will postpone seeing Main Street until later.
4. Take your position at the end of Main Street as follows (on the next page):	Proper positioning will insure that you will be among the first to reach the first ride on the Touring Plan.

117

DIRECTION	EXPLANATION
4a. If you want to ride Space Mountain, turn right at the end of Main Street past the Plaza Restaurant and wait to be admitted at the entrance of the Plaza Pavilion. When the rope barrier is dropped, allowing you to enter Tomorrowland, jog through the Plaza Pavilion and on to Space Mountain. You should be one of the first in to ride.	Space Mountain has long lines all day, except first thing in the morning. Positioning yourself at the entrance to the Plaza Pavilion will give you a hundred-yard head start and a shortcut over anyone proceeding to Space Mountain from the central hub.
4b. If you do not want to ride Space Mountain, wait to be admitted at the central hub. When the rope barrier is dropped, head for Fantasyland via the second bridge on your right as you race counterclockwise around the hub. Go quickly and directly to 20,000 Leagues Under the Sea.	If you are not a roller coaster person, skip Space Mountain and head directly for 20,000 Leagues Under the Sea.
5. If you elected to ride Space Mountain, go now to Fantasyland, keeping the Grand Prix Raceway on your right, and ride 20,000 Leagues Under the Sea. If you skipped Space Mountain, go to Step 6.	20,000 Leagues Under the Sea is the biggest bottleneck in the Magic Kingdom. Unless you get in line within the first 15 to 20 minutes the park is open, you will have a very long wait.
6. While in Fantasyland, ride Snow White's Scary Adventures.	This is a relatively slow-loading ride that will develop long lines later in the day.
7. While in Fantasyland, ride Peter Pan's Flight.	Another slow-loading ride that will develop long lines later in the day.
8. Exit Fantasyland through Cinderella Castle and proceed via	The Jungle Cruise is a well-managed ride; the Disney staff

DIRECTION	EXPLANATION
the central hub to Adventureland. Ride the Jungle Cruise.	do an unusually creditable job of keeping the lines moving.
9. Exiting the Jungle Cruise, turn left and head for Frontierland. Ride Big Thunder Mountain Railroad.	The Touring Plan is arranged to get you to Big Thunder after it has been brought up to full carrying capacity.
10. While in Frontierland, see *Country Bear Jamboree*.	While accessible before noon, *Country Bear Jamboree* builds long lines later in the day.
11. Keeping the waterfront on your left, proceed to Liberty Square and experience the Haunted Mansion.	The Haunted Mansion is a continuous-loading, high-carrying-capacity ride.

NOTE: This is about as far as you can go on a busy day before the crowds catch up with you, but you will have experienced eight or nine of the more popular rides and shows, and you will have cleared almost all of the Magic Kingdom's traffic bottlenecks. Note also that you are doing a considerable amount of walking and some backtracking. Do not be dismayed; the extra walking will save you as much as two hours of standing in line. Remember during the morning (through Step 11), keep moving. In the afternoon, adjust the pace to your liking.

12. Unless you ran into some bad luck you should be within a half hour or less of your 12:15 seating at *Diamond Horseshoe Jamboree* in Frontierland. If you have completed the Touring Plan through Step 11 before noon, go ahead and ride It's a Small World in Fantasyland before you head for the *Jamboree*.	See *Diamond Horseshoe Jamboree* and eat lunch during the show. If you complete Step 11 and still have more than fifteen minutes until your seating, duck into Fantasyland and ride It's a Small World.
If you **did not** make reservations for the Diamond Horseshoe, go ahead and eat lunch at the	The Liberty Tree Tavern is sit-down/full service and will require a longer lunch break than the

DIRECTION	EXPLANATION
Liberty Tree Tavern or wait until after Step 14 and dine at the Adventureland Veranda.	fast-food Adventureland Veranda. Menus with prices are posted outside both.
13. After lunch and the show, go to Liberty Square and see the Hall of Presidents.	This show usually accommodates everyone waiting to see the next performance.
14. Exit Frontierland via the passage to the right of *Diamond Horseshoe Jamboree* and proceed to Adventureland. See *Tropical Serenade (Enchanted Tiki Birds)*.	Once again, everyone waiting is usually admitted.
15. While in Adventureland, ride Pirates of the Caribbean.	This is a high-capacity ride, and you should not experience much of a wait.
16. Return to Frontierland. Catch the Walt Disney World Railroad to Mickey's Birthday-land.	Expect the Frontierland Station to be crowded this time of day. You may not get aboard the first train, but don't worry, another will be along within six minutes.
17. Get off the train at Mickey's Birthdayland. Go to *Mickey's Surprise Party*.	*Mickey's Surprise Party* is a Disney character show that can handle 700-plus people per performance. You should have no trouble getting in. After the show you can go next door to Mickey's Hollywood Theater to meet and photograph Mickey. If this is something you want to do, read the Touring Tips for Mickey's Birthdayland to help you avoid a long wait.
18. Exit Mickey's Birthdayland along the path to Fantasyland. In Fantasyland, see *Magic Journeys*.	A large-capacity theater precludes much of a wait here.

DIRECTION	EXPLANATION
19. While in Fantasyland, ride It's a Small World if you missed it before lunch. Otherwise, proceed to Step 20.	A fast-loading boat ride, where the lines always move quickly.
20. Exit Fantasyland via the Skyway (if the line is not long), or on foot via Cinderella Castle and head for Tomorrowland. Ride Dreamflight.	Dreamflight is a new, fast-loading ride.
21. While in Tomorrowland, ride the WEDway PeopleMover.	Check the crowds waiting for Space Mountain as you ride the PeopleMover.
22. Try *Carousel of Progress*, also in Tomorrowland.	Fast-loading, high-capacity theater ride.
23. Proceeding back toward the entrance of Tomorrowland, experience *Mission to Mars*.	This attraction is very rarely crowded in the late afternoon.
24. Walk across the street and view *American Journeys*.	A large-capacity show, for which your wait should be short.
25. If you have some time left before closing, backtrack to pick up attractions you may have missed, or have bypassed because lines were too long. Check out any parades, fireworks, or live performances that interest you, grab a bite to eat. Save Main Street until last, since it remains open after the rest of the park closes.	
26. Continue to tour until everything closes except Main Street. Finish your day browsing	Main Street is beautiful in the evening with the lights on—it is also very crowded. The shops will

DIRECTION	EXPLANATION
Main Street and viewing *The Walt Disney Story*.	be packed, but it is better to shop at the end of the day than to waste valuable time before you have completed your touring.
27. When you exit the park (assuming you drove your car and must get back to the Transportation and Ticket Center), go to the far ramp of the Monorail Station and board for the Polynesian Resort Hotel. When the monorail doors open at the Transportation and Ticket Center, get out.	Huge crowds mob the monorails bound for the Transportation and Ticket Center from late afternoon through closing time. To avoid these lines, simply take the less crowded monorails servicing the resort hotels. The hotel monorails make all stops including the Transportation and Ticket Center, so it's no problem to get off.

Outline of Magic Kingdom One-Day Touring Plan for Adults

This is the same touring plan that is presented on the preceding pages, only without all of the detail and explanation. If while using this outline version, something is unclear, consult the same step number in the fully elaborated plan.

1. Arrive at the Magic Kingdom parking area one hour before the stated opening time. Purchase your admission.
2. Take the monorail to the Magic Kingdom.
3. Enter the park. Have one person in your party pick up a copy of the daily entertainment schedule at City Hall, while another member of your party makes reservations at the Hospitality House for the 12:15 P.M. seating of *Diamond Horseshoe Jamboree*. Rejoin your party at the Hospitality House.
4. Move quickly to the end of Main Street and (a) take a position at the rope barrier in front of the entrance to the Plaza Pavilion if you want to ride Space Mountain, or (b) if you do not want to ride Space Mountain, take a position at the rope barrier at the central hub. When the barrier is dropped on opening, move quickly to Space Mountain if you chose (a) or to 20,000 Leagues Under the Sea in Fantasyland if you chose (b).
5. If you rode Space Mountain, walk swiftly now to Fantasyland and ride 20,000 Leagues Under the Sea. If you have already ridden 20,000 Leagues, proceed to Step 6.
6. While in Fantasyland, ride Snow White's Scary Adventures.
7. While in Fantasyland, ride Peter Pan's Flight.
8. Exit Fantasyland via the Castle and the central hub. Go to Adventureland and ride the Jungle Cruise.
9. Turn left out of the Jungle Cruise and proceed to Frontierland. Ride Big Thunder Mountain Railroad.
10. While in Frontierland, see *Country Bear Jamboree*.
11. Keeping the waterfront on your left, go to Liberty Square and experience the Haunted Mansion.
12. At this point, you should be within a half hour of your *Diamond*

Horseshoe Jamboree seating at 12:15 P.M. If you have more than 15 minutes before your seating time when you leave the Haunted Mansion, bear left into Fantasyland and ride It's a Small World. Go at 12:15 P.M. to the Jamboree for the show and lunch. If you did not make reservations at the Diamond Horseshoe, eat now at the Liberty Tree Tavern or after Step 14 at the Adventureland Veranda.

13. Go to Liberty Square and see the Hall of Presidents.

14. Return to Frontierland, turning left just after passing *Diamond Horseshoe Jamboree* and take the connecting passage to Adventureland. See *Tropical Serenade (Enchanted Tiki Birds)*.

15. While in Adventureland, ride Pirates of the Caribbean.

16. Exit left and enter Frontierland. Catch the Walt Disney World Railroad to Mickey's Birthdayland.

17. Get off the train at Mickey's Birthdayland. Go to *Mickey's Surprise Party* (enter through Mickey's House).

18. Exit Mickey's Birthdayland via the path to Fantasyland. In Fantasyland, see *Magic Journeys*.

19. While in Fantasyland, ride It's a Small World if you missed it before lunch. Otherwise, proceed to Step 20.

20. Exit Fantasyland via the Skyway (if not too crowded), or on foot via the Castle and the central hub and go to Tomorrowland. Ride Dreamflight.

21. While in Tomorrowland, ride the WEDway PeopleMover.

22. Enjoy *Carousel of Progress*, also in Tomorrowland.

23. Heading back toward the entrance of Tomorrowland, try *Mission to Mars*.

24. Cross the street and see *American Journeys*.

25. If you have any time or energy left catch a live performance, grab a bite, or try any attractions you might have missed using the Touring Plan.

26. Save touring Main Street until last, since it stays open later than the rest of the park. See *The Walt Disney Story*.

27. If you are parked at the Transportation and Ticket Center lot, catch a monorail for the Polynesian Resort Hotel, but get off early when the monorail stops at the Transportation and Ticket Center.

What You Missed

In one day, particularly if the park closes early, it is almost impossible to see and do everything. In the Magic Kingdom One-Day Touring Plan, we have bypassed certain rides and other features that, in our opinion, are expendable if you are on a tight (one-day) schedule. If, however, you are curious about what you would be missing, here's the list:

Main Street:	Main Street Cinema Main Street Vehicles
Adventureland:	Swiss Family Treehouse
Frontierland:	Davy Crockett's Explorer Canoes Tom Sawyer Island Ft. Sam Clemens Frontierland Shootin' Gallery
Mickey's Birthdayland:	Grandma Duck's Petting Farm
Liberty Square:	Mike Fink Keelboats Liberty Square Riverboat
Fantasyland:	Mr. Toad's Wild Ride Cinderella's Golden Carrousel Mad Tea Party Dumbo, the Flying Elephant
Tomorrowland:	Grand Prix Raceway StarJets
Other:	Live shows and parades, etc., for which no reservations are required. These are all worthwhile. Pick up a schedule of shows and activities at City Hall when you enter the park; you may choose to substitute a parade or show for a feature listed on the Touring Plan.

For additional information about rides, shows, and features both included and excluded from this Touring Plan, see "Part Three, The Magic Kingdom."

Outline of Magic Kingdom One-Day Touring Plan, for Parents with Small Children

FOR: **Parents with children between 4 and 8 years of age.**
ASSUMES: Periodic stops for rest, restrooms, and refreshment.

This Touring Plan represents a compromise between the observed tastes of adults and the observed tastes of younger children. Included in this Touring Plan are many amusement park rides which children may have the opportunity to experience (although in less exotic surroundings) at local fairs and amusement parks. Though these rides are included in the Touring Plan, we suggest, nevertheless, that they be omitted if possible. Often requiring long waits in line, these so-called cycle-loading rides consume valuable touring time. Specifically we refer to:

Mad Tea Party   Dumbo, the Flying Elephant
Cinderella's Golden Carrousel   StarJets

This time could be better spent experiencing the many attractions which best demonstrate the Disney creative genius and are only found in the Magic Kingdom.

This Touring Plan is presented in outline form only. For elaboration of the rationale of the different steps see the EXPLANATION column of the Magic Kingdom One-Day Touring Plan, pages 117–122. For critical evaluation of the individual attractions, see "Part Three, The Magic Kingdom," pages 59–100.

Be forewarned that this plan requires a lot of walking and some backtracking; this is necessary to avoid long waits in line. A little extra walking will save you from two to three hours of standing in line. Note also that you may not complete the tour. How far you get will depend on how quickly you move from ride to ride, how many times you pause for rest or food, how quickly and how full the park fills, and what time the park closes. With a little hustle and some luck, it is possible to complete the Touring Plan even on a busy day when the park closes early.

1. Arrive at the main parking lot at least one hour and fifteen minutes before the stated opening time.

2. Take the monorail to the Magic Kingdom.

3. Enter the park. Have one person in your party pick up a copy of the daily entertainment schedule at City Hall, while another member of your party makes reservations at the Hospitality House for the 12:15 seating of *Diamond Horseshoe Jamboree*. Rejoin your party at the Hospitality House.

4. Move quickly to the end of Main Street and take a position at the rope barrier at the central hub. When the barrier is dropped on opening, move quickly to 20,000 Leagues Under the Sea in Fantasyland.

5. While in Fantasyland, ride Mr. Toad's Wild Ride.

6. While in Fantasyland, ride Snow White's Scary Adventures.

7. While in Fantasyland, ride Peter Pan's Flight.

8. While in Fantasyland, ride Dumbo the Flying Elephant.

9. Exit Fantasyland via the Castle and the central hub. Go to Adventureland and ride the Jungle Cruise.

10. Exit left from the Jungle Cruise and go to Frontierland. Ride Big Thunder Mountain Railroad. Not too scary, but kids need to be 3'4" to ride. Strictly enforced. Skip to Step 11 if your children are too small.

11. While in Frontierland, see *Country Bear Jamboree*.

12. Keeping the waterfront on your left, go to Liberty Square and experience the Haunted Mansion.

13. At this point, you should be within a half hour of your *Diamond Horseshoe Jamboree* seating at 12:15 P.M. If you have more than 15 minutes before your seating time when you leave the Haunted Mansion, bear left into Fantasyland and ride It's a Small World. Go at 12:15 P.M. to the *Jamboree* for the show and lunch. If you did not make reservations at *Diamond Horseshoe*, eat now at the Liberty Tree Tavern or before Step 14 at the Adventureland Veranda.

14. Take the passage on the right side of *Diamond Horseshoe* and return to Adventureland. Tour the Swiss Family Treehouse.

15. While in Adventureland, ride Pirates of the Caribbean.

16. Move next door to Frontierland. Take the raft to Tom Sawyer Island. Children will play here all day, so set some limits based on the closing time of the park, your energy level, and how many additional attractions you wish to experience.

17. Return via raft from Tom Sawyer Island and go to the Frontier-land Railroad Station. Catch the Walt Disney World Railroad to Mickey's Birthdayland.

18. Get off the Train at Mickey's Birthdayland. Go to *Mickey's Surprise Party* (enter through Mickey's House), enjoy the play-ground and Grandma Duck's Petting Farm.

19. Exit Mickey's Birthdayland via the path to Fantasyland. In Fantasyland, see *Magic Journeys*.

20. While in Fantasyland, ride It's a Small World if you missed it before lunch. Otherwise, proceed to Step 21.

21. Exit Fantasyland via the Skyway (if not too crowded), or on foot via the Castle and the central hub and go to Tomorrowland. Ride Dreamflight.

22. While in Tomorrowland, ride the WEDway PeopleMover.

23. Enjoy *Carousel of Progress*, also in Tomorrowland.

24. Heading back toward the entrance of Tomorrowland, try *Mission to Mars*.

25. Cross the street and see *American Journeys*.

26. If you have any time or energy left, catch a live performance, grab a bite, or try any attractions you might have missed using the Touring Plan.

27. Save touring Main Street until last, since it stays open later than the rest of the park.

28. If you are parked at the Transportation and Ticket Center lot, catch a monorail for the Polynesian Resort Hotel, but get off early when the monorail stops at the Transportation and Ticket Center.

What You Missed

Listed below is a summary of the rides, shows, and attractions you will not see on this Magic Kingdom One-Day Touring Plan:

Main Street:	*Walt Disney Story*
	Main Street Cinema
	Main Street Vehicles
Adventureland:	*Tropical Serenade*
Frontierland:	Davy Crockett's Explorer Canoes
	Frontierland Shootin' Gallery
	Hall of Presidents

Liberty Square:	Mike Fink Keelboats
Fantasyland:	Cinderella's Golden Carrousel Mad Tea Party
Tomorrowland:	Space Mountain StarJets Grand Prix Raceway
Other:	Live shows and parades, etc., for which no reservations are required. These are all worthwhile. Pick up a schedule of shows and activities at City Hall when you enter the park; you may choose to substitute a parade or show for a feature listed on the Touring Plan.

—— *Not to be Missed at the Magic Kingdom* ——

Adventureland	Jungle Cruise Pirates of the Caribbean
Frontierland	Big Thunder Mountain Railroad *Country Bear Jamboree* *Diamond Horseshoe Jamboree*
Liberty Square	*The Hall of Presidents* The Haunted Mansion
Fantasyland	*It's a Small World* Peter Pan's Flight 20,000 Leagues Under the Sea
Tomorrowland	Space Mountain
Special events	Main Street Electrical Parade

Magic Kingdom Summary

P.O. Box 1000, Lake Buena Vista, FL 32830-1000
Call ahead for opening/closing times
Type: Fantasy/Adventure Theme Park   Phone: (407) 824-4321

Admissions

Ticket options	Discounts	
One-Day Ticket	Children (3–9)	**yes**
3-Day World Passport	Children under 3	**free**
4-Day World Passport	Students	**varies**
5-Day World Passport	Military	**varies**
1-Year World Passport	Senior citizens	**varies**
	Group rates	**yes**

Credit cards accepted for admission: **MasterCard, American Express** and **VISA**.
Features included: **All except Frontierland Shootin' Gallery**

---

*Overall Appeal**

By age groups	Preschool	Grade School	Teens	Young Adults	Over 30	Senior Citizens
	★★★★★	★★★★★	★★★★★	★★★★★	★★★★★	★★★★★

Touring Tips

Touring time
  Average: **Full day**
  Minimum: **Full day**
  Touring strategy: **See narrative**
  Rainy day touring: **Recommended**

Periods of lightest attendance
  Time of day: **Early morning**
  Days: **Friday, Sunday**
  Times of year: **After Thanksgiving**
  until 18th of December

What the Critics Say

Rating of major features:
See pages 63–100

Rating of functional and operational areas

Parking	★★★★★
Restrooms	★★★★★
Resting places	★★★★★
Crowd management	★★★★★
Aesthetic appeal of grounds	★★★★★
Cleanliness/maintenance	★★★★★

Services and Facilities

Restaurant/snack bar **Yes**
Vending machines (food/pop) **No**
Alcoholic beverages **No**
Handicapped access **Yes**
Wheelchairs **Rental**
Baby strollers **Rental**

Lockers **Yes**
Pet kennels **Yes**
Gift shops **Yes**
Film sales **Yes**
Rain check **No**
Private guided group tours **Yes**

---

*Critical ratings are based on a scale of zero to five stars with five stars being the best possible rating.

PART FOUR—EPCOT Center

Contrasting EPCOT Center and the Magic Kingdom

EPCOT Center is more than twice the physical size of the Magic Kingdom, and it has lines every bit as long as those waiting for the Jungle Cruise or Space Mountain. Obviously, visitors must come prepared to do a considerable amount of walking from attraction to attraction within EPCOT Center and a comparable amount of standing in line.

The size and scope of EPCOT Center also means that one can't really see the whole place in one day without skipping an attraction or two and giving other areas a cursory glance. A major difference between the Magic Kingdom and EPCOT Center, however, is that some of the EPCOT attractions can be either lingered over or skimmed, depending on one's personal interest. A good example is the General Motors' World of Motion pavilion consisting of two sections. The first section is a fifteen-minute ride while the second section is a collection of educational walk-through exhibits and mini-theaters. Nearly all visitors opt to take the ride, but many people, due to time constraints or lack of interest, bypass the exhibits.

Generally speaking, the rides at the Magic Kingdom tend to be designed to create an experience of adventure or fantasy. The experiences created in the EPCOT Center attractions tend to be oriented towards education or inspiration.

Some people will find that the attempts at education are superficial; others will want more entertainment and less education. Most visitors are somewhere in between, finding plenty of entertainment **and** education.

In any event, EPCOT Center is more of an adult place than the Magic Kingdom. What it gains in taking a futuristic, visionary, and technological look at the world, it loses, just a bit, in warmth, happiness, and charm.

As in the Magic Kingdom, we have identified several attractions in EPCOT Center as "not to be missed." But part of the enjoyment of a place like EPCOT Center is that there is something for everyone. If you go in a group, no doubt there will be quite a variety of opinions as to which attraction is "best."

—— *Arriving and Getting Oriented* ——

Arriving at EPCOT Center by private automobile is easy and direct. The park has its own parking lot and, unlike the Magic Kingdom, there is no need to take a monorail or ferryboat to reach the entrance. Trams serve the entire EPCOT Center lot, or if you wish you can walk to the front gate. Monorail service does connect EPCOT Center with the Magic Kingdom parking lot, the Magic Kingdom (transfer required), and with the Resort Hotels (transfer also required).

Like the Magic Kingdom, EPCOT Center has theme sections, but only two: Future World and World Showcase. The technological talent of major corporations and the creative talent of Disney Enterprises went into Future World, which represents a look at where man has come from and where he is going. World Showcase, featuring the distinctive landmarks, cuisine, and culture of a number of nations, is meant to be a sort of permanent world's fair.

From the standpoint of finding your way around, however, EPCOT Center is not at all like the Magic Kingdom. The Magic Kingdom is designed so that at nearly any location in the park you feel a part of a very specific environment—Liberty Square, let's say, or Main Street, U.S.A. Each of these environments is visually closed off from other parts of the park to preserve the desired atmosphere. It wouldn't do for the Jungle Cruise to pass the roaring blacktop of the Grand Prix Raceway, for example.

EPCOT Center, by contrast, is visually open. And while it seems strange to see Liberty Hall on the same horizon with the Eiffel Tower, in-park navigation is normally simplified. A possible exception is in Future World where the enormous east and west CommuniCore buildings effectively hide everything on their opposite sides.

While Cinderella Castle is the focal landmark of the Magic Kingdom, Spaceship Earth is the architectural symbol of EPCOT Center. This shiny, 180-foot "geosphere" is visible from almost every point. Like Cinderella Castle, it can help you keep track of where you are in the park. But because it's in a high-traffic location, and because it's not centrally located, it does not make a very good meeting place.

Any of the distinctively designed national pavilions make good meeting places, but be more specific than, "Hey, let's meet in Japan!" That may sound fun and catchy but remember that the national pavilions are mini-towns, with buildings, monuments, gardens, and plazas. You could wander around quite awhile "in Japan" without making connections with your group. Pick out a specific place in Japan, the sidewalk side of the pagoda, for example.

More Information and Help Galore—
WorldKey Information Service

Whether you need more information or assistance or not, you should know about the innovative WorldKey Information Service. It not only may be useful as you visit EPCOT Center, it will also give you some experience dealing with what may be one of the common video systems of the future.

WorldKey is a network of interactive video display terminals—televisions that react when you touch certain parts of the screen.

The WorldKey system, developed by the Bell System and Walt Disney Productions, will provide you with up to forty minutes of information about EPCOT Center, showing maps and pictures, and describing attractions, restaurants, entertainment, guest services, and shops.

Be patient with the WorldKey and it will guide you, step by step, through an explanation of how to use the system—in English or in Spanish (French and German are to be added later). Stick with the program through at least a few steps and you can use the WorldKey to contact an attendant. Via two-way television and hands-free two-way speakers, the WorldKey attendant can answer your questions, make hotel or restaurant reservations, and help find lost children, among other things.

Because the WorldKey system is so novel, a lot of visitors "play" with it as though it were just another video game. For most people this play is actually an educational experience. They are using what could become one of the data retrieval systems of tomorrow. They are learning about touch-sensitive screens. (You don't need to press, by the way; sometimes the system reacts even before your finger touches the screen.)

But whether people play with the WorldKey or put it to work, they usually end up walking away from the screen without completing the WorldKey program and setting it up for the next user. If people get frustrated with the WorldKey it's usually because they walked up to it while it was in the middle of showing the last user what he asked to see.

If, as opposed to finding a program in progress left from a previous user, you initiate the program, the WorldKey will quickly show you, step by step, how to use the system.

If you wish to speak to an attendant, work through the program until a prompt for an attendant is displayed on the screen. Touch the screen as indicated and soon one of the WorldKey attendants will come "live" onto the screen, ready to communicate with you. You can make restaurant reservations at this time and avoid standing in line for reservations at the places themselves.

Future World

Gleaming, futuristic structures of immense proportions leave little in doubt concerning the orientation of this, the first encountered theme area of EPCOT Center. The thoroughfares are broad and punctuated with billowing fountains, reflected in the shining facades of space-age architecture. Everything, including the bountiful landscaping, is clean and sparkling to the point of asepsis and seemingly bigger than life. Pavilions dedicated to man's past, present, and future technological accomplishments form the perimeter of the Future World area with the Spaceship Earth and its flanking CommuniCores East and West standing preeminent front and center.

Spaceship Earth

Type of Ride: Educational journey through past, present, and into the future

When to Go: As soon as the park opens or after 5:30 P.M.

Special Comments: If lines are long when you arrive, try again between 5 and 6 P.M.

Authors' Rating: One of EPCOT's best; ★★★★½

Overall Appeal by Age Group:

Pre-school	Grade School	Teens	Young Adults	Over 30	Senior Citizens
★★★★	★★★★½	★★★★½	★★★★½	★★★★½	★★★★½

Duration of Ride: About 16 minutes

Average Wait in Line per 100 People Ahead of You: 3 minutes

Assumes: 140 or more cars operating

Loading Speed: Moderate to fast

DESCRIPTION AND COMMENTS This Bell System ride spirals through the seventeen-story interior of EPCOT Center's premier landmark, taking visitors past AudioAnimatronics scenes depicting man's developments in communications, from cave painting to printing to television to space communications and computer networks. The ride is compelling and well done as you ascend the geosphere but, to us, a little disappointing on the way back down. Even so, it's a masterpiece and is thus accorded a "not to be missed" rating.

TOURING TIPS   This is probably the toughest attraction in EPCOT Center to see without literally investing hours of your time standing in line. The only way we know to beat the crowd at Spaceship Earth is to be one of the first visitors in the park when it opens. If lines are long when you arrive, try again between 5:30 P.M. and 6:30 P.M. Do not miss it, however, even if you have to stand awhile in line; it's one of Disney's prize achievements.

Earth Station

DESCRIPTION AND COMMENTS   Not an attraction as such. Earth Station is situated at the base of the geosphere and serves as the exit of Spaceship Earth. It also serves as EPCOT Center's primary guest relations and information center. Attendants staff information booths and a number of WorldKey terminals are available. If you have spent any time in the Magic Kingdom, Earth Station is EPCOT Center's version of City Hall.

TOURING TIPS   If you wish to eat in one of the EPCOT Center sit-down restaurants, you can make your reservations from Earth Station through a WorldKey Information Service attendant (instead of running to the restaurant itself and standing in line for reservations, which is another alternative). See the description of the WorldKey system, page 137, and the section dealing with eating in EPCOT Center, page 169.

CommuniCore

Type of Attraction: Multifaceted attraction featuring static and "hands-on" exhibits relating to energy, communications, information processing, and future EPCOT developments

When to Go: On your second day at EPCOT or after you have seen all the major attractions

Special Comments: Most exhibits demand some time and participation to be rewarding; not much to be gained here in a quick walk-through.

Authors' Rating: Interesting on the whole, though not particularly compelling. *Rollercoaster* (you design your own roller coaster with the assistance of a computer) in EPCOT Computer Central (Communicore East) is our pick of the litter.

Overall Appeal by Age Group:

Pre-school	Grade School	Teens	Young Adults	Over 30	Senior Citizens
★★	★★	★★	★★½	★★½	★★½

DESCRIPTION AND COMMENTS   The name stands for "Community Core," and it consists of two huge, crescent-shaped, glass-walled structures housing industry-sponsored walk-through and "hands-on" exhibits, restaurants, and a gift shop. The Disney people like to describe it as a "twenty-first-century village square where the town crier is an array of computer-fed, interactive video screens and high technology electronics libraries."

TOURING TIPS   CommuniCore (two buildings: east and west) provides visitors an opportunity to sample a variety of technology in a fun, "hands-on" manner through the use of various interactive communication devices. Some of the exhibits are quite intriguing while others are a little dry. We observed a wide range of reactions by visitors to the many CommuniCore exhibits and can only suggest that you form your own opinion. In terms of touring strategy, we suggest you spend time in CommuniCore on your second day at EPCOT Center. If you only have one day, visit sometime during the evening if you have time. Be warned, however, that CommuniCore exhibits are almost all technical and educational in nature and may not be compatible with your mood or level of energy toward the end of a long day of touring. Also be advised that you cannot get much of anything out of a quick walk-through of CommuniCore; you have to play with the equipment to understand what is going on.

Attractions in CommuniCore East include:

EPCOT Computer Central

DESCRIPTION AND COMMENTS   Touch-sensitive video terminals show users through simple and entertaining games how computers are used in design and control. A robot called SMRT-1 plays guessing games with guests by decoding yes and no answers through a voice recognition box.

TOURING TIPS   See comments in CommuniCore Touring Tips.

Travelport

DESCRIPTION AND COMMENTS   This American Express exhibit in CommuniCore East has "vacation stations" equipped with touch-sensitive video terminals similar to those in the WorldKey system. If you work with a terminal you can see different types of vacations in different geographical areas.

TOURING TIPS   See comments in CommuniCore Touring Tips.

Energy Exchange

DESCRIPTION AND COMMENTS   There are also touch-sensitive video terminals in this Exxon exhibit, permitting users to tap into information about a variety of energy topics. Stationary displays are devoted to specific energy sources—solar, coal, nuclear, oil, and others. Visitors can use some of the devices to demonstrate the generation and expenditure of energy.

TOURING TIPS   See comments in CommuniCore Touring Tips.

Electronic Forum

DESCRIPTION AND COMMENTS   This section of CommuniCore consists of World News Center, which has TV monitors carrying live news broadcasts from around the world. At Future Choice Theater visitors can participate in an on-going opinion poll by pushing buttons built into the armrests of their seats. Responses appear on the theater screen so guests can see how their opinions stack up against those of other visitors.

TOURING TIPS   See comments in CommuniCore Touring Tips.

Backstage Magic

DESCRIPTION AND COMMENTS   This Sperry exhibit gives visitors a look through the windows of the EPCOT Center Computer Control Room.

TOURING TIPS   This exhibit is produced in a small theater, so there is almost always a minimum wait in line of twenty minutes. The show is not particularly compelling or informative; one of EPCOT Center's less appealing offerings in our opinion.

Attractions in CommuniCore West include:

FutureCom

DESCRIPTION AND COMMENTS   A Bell System exhibit with a variety of electronic games demonstrating facets of telecommunications. Another part of the exhibit demonstrates video teleconferencing, putting visitors face-to-face via two-way television with an attendant. Still another section has touch-sensitive video terminals that enable guests to "call up" information on any U.S. state and its current events.

TOURING TIPS   See additional comments in CommuniCore Touring Tips.

EPCOT Outreach

DESCRIPTION AND COMMENTS   EPCOT Outreach consists of static displays illustrating various EPCOT projects and developments, and a library service that provides information on demand concerning any topic presented in either Future World or World Showcase.

TOURING TIPS   This is where someone will try to answer that question you have been kicking around all day. If you are an educator with a group, special tour-enhancing handouts can be obtained here.

The Living Seas

Type of Attraction: Multifaceted attraction consisting of an underwater ride beneath a huge saltwater aquarium and a number of exhibits and displays dealing with oceanography and ocean ecology and sea life.

When to Go: Before 10 A.M. or after 3 P.M.

Special Comments: The ride is only a small component of this attraction. See description and touring tips below for information on the rest of the attraction.

Authors' Rating: The Living Seas will improve as the specimen population in its main tank grows; ★★★★

Overall Appeal by Age Group:

Pre-school	Grade School	Teens	Young Adults	Over 30	Senior Citizens
★★★	★★★½	★★★½	★★★★	★★★★	★★★★

Duration of Ride: 3 minutes

Average Wait in Line per 100 People Ahead of You: 3½ minutes

Assumes: All elevators in operation

Loading Speed: Fast

DESCRIPTION AND COMMENTS   The Living Seas is one of the most ambitious Future World offerings. The focus is a huge, 200-foot diameter, 27-foot-deep main tank containing approximately 6,000 fish, mammals, and crustaceans in a simulation of a real ocean ecosystem. Scientists and divers conduct actual marine experiments underwater in view of EPCOT Center guests. Visitors can view the undersea activity through 8-inch-thick viewing windows below the surface (including viewing windows in the Coral Reef Restaurant), and via a three-part adventure/ride which is the featured attraction of The Living Seas. This last consists of a movie dramatizing the link between the ocean and man's survival followed by an elevator descent to the bottom of the tank. Here guests board gondolas for a three-minute voyage through an underwater viewing tunnel.

At present, the fish population of the Living Seas main tank appears a little sparse, and the underwater ride is over almost before you have gotten comfortably situated in the gondola. But, no matter, the strength of this attraction lies in the dozen or so exhibits offered after the ride. Visitors can view aqua culture fish-breeding experiments, watch short films about various forms of sea life, and much more. You can stay as long as you wish in the exhibit area.

The Living Seas is a high-quality marine/aquarium exhibit, but is no substitute for visiting Sea World, an enormous marine life theme park every bit on a par in terms of quality, appeal, educational value, and entertainment with either the Magic Kingdom or EPCOT Center.

TOURING TIPS   Go before 10 A.M. or after 3 P.M. You can save about ten minutes of time by being among the last to go from the pre-show area (where you stand to watch a short slide show) into the theater where you sit to view a film. Facing the screen, sit as far to the right as possible in the theater.

The Land

DESCRIPTION AND COMMENTS The Land is in fact a huge pavilion sponsored by Kraft which contains three attractions (discussed next) and a number of restaurants.

TOURING TIPS The Land is a good place for a fast-food lunch; if you are there to see the attraction, however, don't go during meal times.

Attractions in The Land Include:

Listen to the Land

Type of Ride: A boat ride/adventure through the past, present and future of U.S. farming and agriculture.

When to Go: Before 10:30 A.M. or after 7:30 P.M.

Special Comments: Take this ride early in the morning but save the other Land attractions for later in the day. Located on the lower level of The Land pavilion

Authors' Rating: Interesting and fun; ★★★★★

Overall Appeal by Age Group:

Pre-school	Grade School	Teens	Young Adults	Over 30	Senior Citizens
★★★	★★★★	★★★★	★★★★★	★★★★★	★★★★★

Duration of Ride: About 12 minutes

Average Wait in Line per 100 People Ahead of You: 3 minutes

Assumes: 15 boats operating

Loading Speed: Moderate

DESCRIPTION AND COMMENTS A boat ride which takes visitors through a simulated giant seed germination, past various inhospitable environments man has faced as a farmer, and through a futuristic, innovative greenhouse where real crops are being grown using the latest agricultural technologies. Inspiring and educational with excellent effects and a good narrative, this attraction should "not be missed."

TOURING TIPS This "not to be missed" attraction should be seen before the lunch crowd hits The Land restaurants, i.e., before 10:30 A.M., or in the evening after 7:30 P.M.

Kitchen Kabaret

Type of Show: AudioAnimatronic variety show about food and nutrition

When to Go: Before 11 A.M. or after 3 P.M.

Special Comments: Located on the lower level of The Land pavilion

Authors' Rating: Lively and amusing; ★★★½

Overall Appeal by Age Group:

Pre-school	Grade School	Teens	Young Adults	Over 30	Senior Citizens
★★★★	★★★★	★★★	★★★½	★★★½	★★★★

Duration of Presentation: Approximately 13 minutes

Pre-Show Entertainment: None

Probable Waiting Time: Less than 10 minutes

DESCRIPTION AND COMMENTS Disney AudioAnimatronic (robotic) characters in the forms of various foods and kitchen appliances take the stage in an educational musical revue, which tells the story of the basic food groups (protein, carbohydrates, etc.). It's a cute show with entertainment provided by such characters as Bonnie Appetit, the Cereal Sisters, and the comedy team of Mr. Hamm and Mr. Eggz.

TOURING TIPS One of the few light entertainment offerings at EPCOT Center. Slightly reminiscent of the *Country Bear Jamboree* in the Magic Kingdom (but not quite as humorous or endearing in our opinion). Though the theater is not large, we have never encountered any long waits at the *Kitchen Kabaret* (even during meal times). Nevertheless, we recommend you go before 11 A.M. or after 3 P.M.

Harvest Theater: Symbiosis

Type of Show: Film exploring man's relationship with his environment

When to Go: Before 11 A.M. and after 3 P.M.

Authors' Rating: Extremely interesting and enlightening; ★★★★

Overall Appeal by Age Group:

Pre-school	Grade School	Teens	Young Adults	Over 30	Senior Citizens
★★½	★★★	★★★½	★★★½	★★★★	★★★½

Duration of Presentation: Approximately 18½ minutes

Pre-Show Entertainment: None
Probable Waiting Time: 10–15 minutes

DESCRIPTION AND COMMENTS   This attraction features a 70mm Pana-vision film, *Symbiosis*. The subject is the interrelationship of man and his environment, and demonstrates how easily man can upset the eco-logical balance. The film is superb in its production and not too heavy-handed in its sobering message. The cinematic technique is "state of the art."

TOURING TIPS   This extremely worthwhile film should be part of every visitor's touring day. Long waits are usually not a problem at the Harvest Theater, but as with *Kitchen Kabaret*, we recommend you go before 11 A.M. or after 3 P.M.

Journey into Imagination

DESCRIPTION AND COMMENTS   Another multi-attraction pavilion, lo-cated on the west side of CommuniCore West and down the walk from The Land. Outside is an "upside-down waterfall" and one of our favorite Future World landmarks, the so-called "jumping water," a leap-frogging fountain that seems to hop over the heads of unsuspecting passers-by.

TOURING TIPS   We recommend early morning or late evening touring. See the individual attractions for further specifics.

Attractions in Journey into Imagination include:

Journey into Imagination Ride

Type of Ride: Fantasy adventure
When to Go: Before 10:30 A.M. or after 7 P.M.
Authors' Rating: Lighthearted and happy; ★★★★
Overall Appeal by Age Group:

Pre-school	Grade School	Teens	Young Adults	Over 30	Senior Citizens
★★★★	★★★★	★★★½	★★★½	★★★½	★★★½

Duration of Ride: Approximately 13 minutes
Average Wait in Line per 100 People Ahead of You: 3 minutes

Assumes: 20 trains operating

Loading Speed: Moderate to fast

DESCRIPTION AND COMMENTS   This ride introduces two new Disney characters—Figment, an impish purple dragon, and Dreamfinder, a red-bearded adventurer who pilots a contraption designed to search out and capture ideas. This ride, with its happy, humorous orientation and superb AudioAnimatronics and special effects, is one of the most fun and delightful attractions in the park. It is "not to be missed."

TOURING TIPS   This "not to be missed" ride is the big draw in this corner of Future World. We recommend seeing it before 10:30 A.M., or alternatively after 7 P.M.

The Image Works

Type of Attraction: Hands-on creative playground employing color, music, touch-sensation, and electronic devices

When to Go: Immediately after taking the Journey into Imagination Ride

Special Comments: You do not have to wait in the long line for the ride in this pavilion to gain access to The Image Works. Simply go through the open door just to the left of where the line for the ride is entering. You will not have a wait.

Authors' Rating: A fun change of pace; be sure to see the Dreamfinder's School of Drama; ★★★½

Overall Appeal by Age Group:

Pre-school	Grade School	Teens	Young Adults	Over 30	Senior Citizens
★★★★	★★★★	★★★★	★★★★	★★★½	★★★½

Probable Waiting Time: No waiting required

DESCRIPTION AND COMMENTS   This is a playground for the imagination utilizing light, color, sound, and electronic devices which can be manipulated by visitors. There's the Magic Palette, with a video-screen canvas and an electronic paintbrush. Especially fun is the Electronic Philharmonic, which enables visitors to conduct the brass, woodwind, percussion, and string sections of an orchestra by movements of the hand. (The secret is raising and lowering your hands over the labeled discs on the console. Don't try pressing the discs as if they were buttons. Pretend you're a conductor—raise a hand away from the disc labeled brass, for example, and you will get louder brass. Lower your hand toward the disc labeled woodwinds and you'll get less volume from the woodwinds section.)

TOURING TIPS   There are quite a number of interesting things to do and play with here, far more than the representative examples we listed. If you have more than one day at EPCOT Center, save The Image Works for the second day. If you are on a one-day schedule, try to work it in during the evening or late afternoon.

Magic Eye Theater: Captain EO

Type of Show: 3-D rock and roll space fantasy film
When to Go: Before 11 A.M. or after 5 P.M.
Special Comments: Adults should not be put off by the rock music or sci-fi theme. They will enjoy the show as much as the kids do.
Authors' Rating: An absolute hoot! Not to be missed; ★★★★
Overall Appeal by Age Group:

Pre-school	Grade School	Teens	Young Adults	Over 30	Senior Citizens
★★★★★	★★★★★	★★★★★	★★★★½	★★★★½	★★★★

Duration of Presentation: Approximately 17 minutes
Pre-Show Entertainment: 8 minutes
Probable Waiting Time: 12 minutes (at suggested times)

DESCRIPTION AND COMMENTS   *Captain EO* is sort of the ultimate rock video. Starring Michael Jackson and directed by Francis Coppola, the 3-D space fantasy is more than a film; it is a happening. Action on the screen is augmented by lasers, fiber-optics, cannons, and a host of other special effects in the theater, as well as by some audience participation. There's not much of a story, but there's plenty of music and dancing performed by some of the most unlikely creatures ever to shake a tail feather.

TOURING TIPS   As a new attraction, *Captain EO* draws large crowds. During the summer and holiday periods when there are large numbers of kids in the park, it's best to see *Captain EO* before 10:30 A.M.

The World of Motion

DESCRIPTION AND COMMENTS   Presented by General Motors, this pavilion is to the left of Spaceship Earth when you enter and down toward World Showcase from the Universe of Energy pavilion. The pavilion is home to It's Fun to Be Free, a ride, and to TransCenter, an assembly of stationary exhibits and mini-theater productions on the theme of transportation.

Attractions in The World of Motion include:

It's Fun to Be Free

Type of Ride: AudioAnimatronic survey of the history of transportation

When to Go: Any time except between noon and 2 P.M.

Special Comments: Nearby Universe of Energy discharges its audiences en masse causing temporary congestion at both next-door Horizons and The World of Motion

Authors' Rating: Not to be missed; ★★★★★

Overall Appeal by Age Group:

Pre-school	Grade School	Teens	Young Adults	Over 30	Senior Citizens
★★★★	★★★★★	★★★★	★★★★★	★★★★★	★★★★★

Duration of Ride: Approximately 14½ minutes

Average Wait in Line per 100 People Ahead of You: 2¾ minutes

Assumes: Normal operation

Loading Speed: Moderate to fast

DESCRIPTION AND COMMENTS   A "not-to-be-missed" attraction, this ride conducts visitors through a continuum of twenty-four AudioAnimatronics scenes depicting where and how man has traveled, and what the future has in store for travel. The detail-work in individual scenes is amazing and the tongue-in-cheek, humorous tone of the ride makes the history lesson more than tolerable.

TOURING TIPS   This ride has a large carrying capacity and an efficient loading system, keeping lines generally manageable. Many days you can hop on this ride any time you want. Its largest crowds build between noon and 2 P.M. and immediately after an audience has been discharged from Universe of Energy nearby.

TransCenter

Type of Attraction: Exhibits and mini-theater productions concerning the evolution and future of transportation, particularly as relates to the automobile

When to Go: On your second day or after you've seen the major attractions

Special Comments: World of Motion is the only pavilion with a separate entrance to its exhibit area, making visitation possible at a time other than when you take the It's Fun to Be Free ride.

Authors' Rating: Informative with a healthy dose of humor; ★★★

Overall Appeal by Age Group:

Pre-school	Grade School	Teens	Young Adults	Over 30	Senior Citizens
★★½	★★★	★★★	★★★	★★★	★★★

Probable Waiting Time: No waiting required if you enter through the rear entrance

DESCRIPTION AND COMMENTS   Most visitors enter TransCenter when they disembark from the ride described above, but there are separate doors on the east side of the pavilion for those who wish to visit the various exhibits without taking the ride. TransCenter is a walk-through attraction of 33,000 square feet, and deals with a wide range of topics relating to transportation. One major display demonstrates the importance of aerodynamics to fuel economy, while others evaluate the prospects of future power systems and explains why the industry is turning to robotic production techniques. Yet another display, Dreamers' Workshop, shows some advanced designs for the possible land, sea, and air conveyances of tomorrow.

TOURING TIPS   There's a lot to see here. How much you take in will be determined by your interest in the subject and the flexibility of your schedule. We like TransCenter on the second day of a two-day visit, or during the mid-afternoon if you enjoy this sort of display more than the offerings of World Showcase. Late evening after you have finished your "must list" is also a good time.

Horizons

Type of Ride: A look at man's evolving perception of the future

When to Go: Before 10:30 A.M. or after 3:30 P.M.

Special Comments: Periodically inundated when the Universe of Energy, next door, discharges an audience

Authors' Rating: Not to be missed; ★★★★½

Overall Appeal by Age Group:

Pre-school	Grade School	Teens	Young Adults	Over 30	Senior Citizens
★★★★	★★★★	★★★★	★★★★½	★★★★½	★★★★½

Duration of Ride: Approximately 15 minutes

Average Wait in Line per 100 People Ahead of You: 4 minutes

Assumes: Normal operation

Loading Speed: Moderate to fast

DESCRIPTION AND COMMENTS   The General Electric pavilion takes a look back at yesterday's visions of the future, including Jules Verne's concept of a moon rocket and a 1930s preview of a neon city. Elsewhere guests visit FuturePort and ride through a family habitat of the next century, with scenes depicting apartment, farm, and underwater and space communities.

TOURING TIPS   The entire Horizons pavilion is devoted to a single, continuously loading ride, which has a large carrying capacity. This "not to be missed" attraction can be enjoyed almost any time of day without long waits in line. An exception occurs immediately following the conclusion of a Universe of Energy performance next door, when up to 580 patrons often troop over and queue up for Horizons en masse. If you chance to encounter this deluge or its aftermath, take a 15-minute break. Chances are when you return to Horizons you will be able to walk right in.

Wonders Of Life *(opens 1989)*

DESCRIPTION AND COMMENTS   Presented by the Metropolitan Life Insurance Company, this newest addition to the Future World family is a multifaceted pavilion dealing with the human body, health, and medicine. Housed in a 100,000-square-foot, gold-domed structure, Wonders of Life will house a variety of attractions focusing on the capabilities of the human body and the importance of keeping it fit.

Attractions in Wonders of Life include:

Body Wars

Type of Ride: Flight simulator ride through the human body
When to Go: As soon as possible after the park opens
Special Comments: Not recommended for pregnant women or for those prone to motion sickness.
Authors' Rating: Absolutely mindblowing, not to be missed; ★★★★★
Projected Overall Appeal by Age Group:

Pre-school	Grade School	Teens	Young Adults	Over 30	Senior Citizens
★★★★★	★★★★★	★★★★★	★★★★★	★★★★★	★★★★★

Duration of Ride: A little over six minutes
Average Wait in Line per 100 People Ahead of You: 4 minutes
Assumes: four simulators operating
Loading Speed: Fast

DESCRIPTION AND COMMENTS   This is a thrill ride through the immune system of the human body, developed in the image of the Star Tours space simulation ride. The plot is a life-and-death race against time to save the life of a man. The simulator creates a vividly realistic experience as guests seem to hurtle at fantastic speeds through anatomical images as the body fights disease. The sights are as mind-boggling as the ride is breathtaking, in this "not to be missed" attraction.

TOURING TIPS   This is EPCOT Center's first and only thrill ride and is popular with all age groups. Catch it as soon as possible after the park opens.

Cranium Command

Type of Show: Audio-Animatronic character show about the brain
When to Go: Before 11 A.M. or after 3 P.M.
Author's Rating: Funny, outrageous, and educational; ★★★★
Projected Overall Appeal by Age Group:

Pre-school	Grade School	Teens	Young Adults	Over 30	Senior Citizens
★★★★½	★★★★½	★★★★	★★★★½	★★★★½	★★★★½

Duration of Presentation: Approximately 13 minutes
Pre-Show Entertainment: Pending
Probable Waiting Time: Less than ten minutes at touring times
    suggested.

DESCRIPTION AND COMMENTS   A humorous and enlightening look at the mind's relationship with all the other body systems. Combining special effects and motion pictures, the theater production will feature new Disney AudioAnimatronic characters called "Brain Pilots."

TOURING TIPS   We recommend you go before 11 A.M. or after 3 P.M.

Fitness Fairgrounds

DESCRIPTION AND COMMENTS   Much of the pavilion's interior is devoted to an assortment of visitor participation exhibits, where guests can test their senses in a fun house, receive computer-generated health analyses of their personal lifestyles, work out on electronically sophisticated exercise equipment, watch a video presentation called "Goofy About Health" (starring who else?), and view a film on human development and birth.

TOURING TIPS   We recommend you save the Fitness Fair exhibits for your second day, or the end of your first day at EPCOT Center.

Universe of Energy

Type of Attraction: Combination ride/theater presentation about
    energy
When to Go: Before 10:30 A.M. or after 4:30 P.M.
Special Comments: Do not be dismayed by large lines; 580 people
    disappear into the pavilion each time the theater turns over.
Authors' Rating: One of EPCOT's premier presentations; ★★★★★
Overall Appeal by Age Group:

Pre-school	Grade School	Teens	Young Adults	Over 30	Senior Citizens
★★★★★	★★★★★	★★★★★	★★★★★	★★★★★	★★★★★

Duration of Presentation: Approximately 26½ minutes
Pre-Show Entertainment: 8 minutes
Probable Waiting Time: 20–40 minutes

DESCRIPTION AND COMMENTS   The AudioAnimatronic dinosaurs and the unique traveling theater make this Exxon pavilion one of the most popular in Future World. Since this is a theater with a ride component, the line does not move at all while the show is in progress. When the theater empties, however, a large chunk of the line will disappear as people are admitted for the next show. At this "not to be missed" attraction, visitors are seated in what appears to be a fairly ordinary theater while they watch an animated film on fossil fuels. Then, the theater seats divide into six 97-passenger traveling cars which glide among the swamps and reptiles of a prehistoric forest. The special effects include the feel of warm, clammy air from the swamp, the smell of sulphur from an erupting volcano, and the sight of red lava hissing and bubbling towards the passengers. The remainder of the performance utilizes some nifty cinematic techniques to bring you back to the leading edge of energy research and development.

TOURING TIPS   This "not to be missed" attraction draws large crowds beginning early in the morning. Either catch the show before 10:30 A.M. or wait until after 4:30 P.M. Waits for the Universe of Energy are normally within tolerable limits, however, since the Universe of Energy contains two separate theaters which can be operated simultaneously.

World Showcase

The second theme component of EPCOT Center is World Showcase. Situated around picturesque World Showcase Lagoon, it is an ongoing world's fair, with the cuisine, culture, history, and architecture of almost a dozen countries permanently on display in individual national pavilions. The so-called pavilions, which generally consist of familiar landmarks and typically representative street scenes from the host country, are spaced along a 1.2-mile promenade which circles the impressive forty-acre lagoon. Double-decker omnibuses carry visitors to stops around the promenade, and boats ferry guests across the lagoon (the lines at the bus stops tend to be pushy, however, and it's almost always quicker to walk than to use the buses or the boats). Moving clockwise around the promenade, the nations represented are:

Mexico

DESCRIPTION AND COMMENTS Two pre-Colombian pyramids dominate the architecture of this exhibit. The first makes up the facade of the pavilion and the second overlooks the restaurant and plaza alongside the boat ride, El Rio del Tiempo, inside the pavilion.

El Rio del Tiempo, The River of Time, is a boat trip which winds among AudioAnimatronics and cinematic scenes depicting the history of Mexico from the ancient cultures of the Maya, Toltec, and Aztec civilizations to modern times. Special effects include fiber-optic projections that provide a spectacular fireworks display near the end of the ride.

TOURING TIPS A romantic and exciting testimony to the charms of Mexico, this pavilion probably contains more authentic and valuable artifacts and objets d'art than any other national pavilion. Many people zip right past these treasures, unfortunately, without even stopping to look. The village scene on the interior of the pavilion is both beautiful and exquisitely detailed. We recommend seeing this pavilion before 11 A.M. or after 7 P.M.

Attractions in Mexico include:

El Rio del Tiempo

Type of Ride: Boat ride
When to Go: Before 11 A.M. or after 7:00 P.M.
Authors' Rating: Light and relaxing; ★★★½
Overall Appeal by Age Group:

Pre-school	Grade School	Teens	Young Adults	Over 30	Senior Citizens
★★★½	★★★½	★★★	★★★½	★★★½	★★★½

Duration of Ride: Approximately 7 minutes (plus 1½-minute wait to disembark)
Average Wait in Line per 100 People Ahead of You: 4½ minutes
Assumes: 16 boats in operation
Loading Speed: Moderate

Norway

DESCRIPTION AND COMMENTS   A very different addition to the World Showcase international pavilions, the Norwegian Pavilion is complex, beautiful, and architecturally diverse. There is a courtyard surrounded by an assortment of traditional Scandinavian buildings including a replica of the 14th-century Akershus Castle, a wooden stave church, red-tiled cottages, and replicas of historic buildings representing the traditional designs of Bergen, Ålesund, and Oslo. Attractions in Norway include an adventure boat ride in the mold of Pirates of the Caribbean, followed by a movie about Norway, and, in the stave church, a gallery of art and artifacts. Located between China and Mexico, the Norway Pavilion houses the Akershus Restaurant, a reservations/sit-down eatery featuring koldtboard (cold buffet) plus a variety of hot Norwegian fare. For those on the run there is an open-air café and a bakery. For shoppers there is an abundance of native handicrafts.

Attractions in Norway include:

Maelstrom

Type of Ride: Disney adventure boat ride
When to Go: Before 10 A.M. or after 3 P.M.

Authors' Rating: One of EPCOT Center's most fun rides; not to be missed; ★★★★★

Overall Appeal by Age Group:

Pre-school	Grade School	Teens	Young Adults	Over 30	Senior Citizens
★★★★	★★★★★	★★★★★	★★★★★	★★★★★	★★★★★

Duration of Ride: About 4½ minutes, followed by a five-minute film with a short wait in between; about 14 minutes for the whole show.

Average Wait in Line per 100 People Ahead of You: 4 minutes

Assumes: Twelve or thirteen boats operating

Loading Speed: Fast

DESCRIPTION AND COMMENTS   Guests board dragon-headed ships for an adventure voyage through the fabled rivers and seas of Viking history and legend. In one of Disney's most ambitious water rides, guests brave trolls, rocky gorges, waterfalls, and a storm at sea. A new-generation Disney water ride, the Viking voyage assembles an impressive array of special effects, combining visual, tactile, and auditory stimuli in a fast-paced and often humorous odyssey. After the ride guests are shown a short (five-minute) film on Norway. We rate this ride as "not to be missed."

TOURING TIPS   A high-capacity, fast-loading attraction. Visitors can expect long but rapidly moving lines. If you have been to EPCOT Center before, you may want to ride at 9 A.M. when World Showcase opens. If you are attempting a comprehensive tour, ride in the mid to late afternoon.

People's Republic of China

DESCRIPTION AND COMMENTS   A half-sized replica of the Temple of Heaven in Beijing (Peking) identifies this pavilion. Gardens and reflecting ponds simulate those found in Suzhou, and an art gallery features a "Lotus Blossom" gate and formal saddleridge roof line.

Pass through the Hall of Prayer for Good Harvest to see the Circle-Vision 360 motion picture, *Wonders of China.* Warm and appealing, the film serves as a brilliant introduction to the people and natural beauty of this little-known nation. Two restaurants have been added to the China pavilion since its opening, a fast-food eatery and a lovely, reservations-only, full-service establishment.

TOURING TIPS   A truly beautiful pavilion, serene yet exciting. We recommend that you tour any time at your convenience.

We recommend the same visitation times for the *Wonders of China*, an excellent film, as for the pavilion in general.

Attractions in People's Republic of China include:

Wonders of China

Type of Show: Film essay on the Chinese people and country
When to Go: Anytime
Special Comments: Audience stands throughout performance
Authors' Rating: Charming and enlightening; ★★★★½
Overall Appeal by Age Group:

Pre-school	Grade School	Teens	Young Adults	Over 30	Senior Citizens
★★★	★★★½	★★★½	★★★★½	★★★★½	★★★★

Duration of Presentation: Approximately 19 minutes
Pre-Show Entertainment: None
Probable Waiting Time: 10 minutes

Germany

DESCRIPTION AND COMMENTS   A clocktower adorned with boy and girl figures overlooks the platz, or plaza, which identifies the pavilion of the Federal Republic of Germany. Dominated by a fountain depicting St. George's victory over the dragon, the platz is encircled by buildings reflecting traditional German architecture. A future ride attraction will take visitors through Germany's interconnecting river system of the Rhine, Tauber, Ruhr, and Isar. For the moment, however, the focal attraction is the Biergarten, a full-service (reservations only) restaurant featuring German food and beer. At evening meals only, yodeling, German folk dancing, singing, and oompah band music accompany the fare.

TOURING TIPS   The pavilion is pleasant and festive. Until the river ride is completed Germany is recommended for touring at any time of the day.

Italy

DESCRIPTION AND COMMENTS   The entrance to the Italian pavilion is marked by the 105-foot campanile, or bell tower, said to be a mirror image of the tower that overlooks St. Mark's Square in Venice. To the left of the campanile is a replica of the fourteenth-century Doge's Palace, also a Venetian landmark. Other buildings are composites of architecture found throughout Italy. The style is Florentine, for example, for L'Originale Alfredo di Roma Ristorante. Visitors can watch pasta being made in this popular restaurant which specializes in Fettuccine All'Alfredo. The Italian pavilion even has a small Venetian island with gondolas tied to barber-pole-striped moorings at the edge of the World Showcase Lagoon.

TOURING TIPS   The streets and courtyards in the Italian pavilion are among the most realistic in World Showcase—you really feel as if you have been transplanted to Italy. Since there is no attraction (film, ride, etc.) at the Italian pavilion, touring is recommended for all hours.

United States

DESCRIPTION AND COMMENTS   The United States pavilion, generally referred to as *The American Adventure* for the historical production performed there, consists of (typically) a fast-food restaurant and a patriotic, AudioAnimatronics show.

The American Adventure is a composite of everything the Disney people do best. Situated in an almost life-size replica of Philadelphia's Liberty Hall, the production is a stirring, twenty-nine-minute rendition of American history narrated by the AudioAnimatronic figures of Mark Twain (who carries a smoking cigar) and Ben Franklin (who climbs a set of stairs to visit Thomas Jefferson). Behind a stage that's almost half the size of a football field is a 28 × 155-foot, rear-projection screen (the largest ever used) on which appropriate motion picture images are interwoven with the action occurring on stage. Definitely a "not to be missed" attraction.

TOURING TIPS   Large and patriotic, but not as interesting externally as most of the other pavilions. The Liberty Inn restaurant is one of the few places in the World Showcase to obtain a quick, fast-food meal.

The American Adventure is, in the opinion of our research team, the very best attraction at EPCOT Center. It usually plays to capacity audiences from around noon through 3:30 P.M., so try to see it early or late. Because of the theater's large capacity, waiting during the busy times of the day would hardly ever approach an hour, and would probably average twenty-five to forty minutes.

Attractions in The United States include:

The American Adventure

Type of Show: Patriotic mixed-media and AudioAnimatronic presentation on U.S. history

When to Go: Before noon and after 3:30 P.M.

Authors' Rating: Possibly the best attraction at EPCOT Center; not to be missed; ★★★★★

Overall Appeal by Age Group:

Pre-school	Grade School	Teens	Young Adults	Over 30	Senior Citizens
★★★	★★★★	★★★★	★★★★½	★★★★★	★★★★★

Duration of Presentation: Approximately 29 minutes

Pre-Show Entertainment: None regularly scheduled

Probable Waiting Time: 16 minutes

Japan

DESCRIPTION AND COMMENTS   The five-story, blue-roofed pagoda, inspired by a shrine built in Nara in the seventh century, sets this pavilion apart from its neighbors. A hill garden rises behind it with arrangements of waterfalls, rocks, flowers, lanterns, paths, and rustic bridges. The building on the right (as one faces the entrance) was inspired by the ceremonial and coronation hall on the Imperial Palace Grounds at Kyoto. It contains restaurants and a large retail store. Passing through the courtyard, one crosses a moat and enters a massive Samurai "castle" that will house Meet the World. This attraction, in which the audience seating area will revolve around the stage, will feature Audio-Animatronic characters in settings that depict Japan's history and spirit.

TOURING TIPS   A tasteful and elaborate pavilion which creatively blends simplicity, architectural grandeur, and natural beauty, Japan can be toured at any time of day.

Morocco

DESCRIPTION AND COMMENTS The bustle of the market, narrow, winding streets, lofty minarets, and stuccoed archways recreate the romance and intrigue of Tangiers and Casablanca. Attention to detail makes Morocco one of the most exciting of the World Showcase pavilions. In addition to the bazaar, Morocco also features a museum of Moorish art and the Marrakech Restaurant, which serves some unusual and difficult-to-find North African ethnic specialities.

TOURING TIPS Since there is no ride or theater attraction in Morocco, it can be toured anytime at your convenience.

France

DESCRIPTION AND COMMENTS Naturally there is a replica of the Eiffel Tower (and a big one at that), but the rest of the pavilion is meant to reflect a more general ambience of France in the period 1870 to 1910, a period known as La Belle Epoque (the beautiful time). The sidewalk cafe and the restaurant are both very popular here, but so is the pastry shop. You won't be the first visitor to get the idea of buying a croissant to tide you over until you can obtain a decent meal.

Impressions de France is the name of an eighteen-minute movie which is projected over 200 degrees onto five screens. They let you sit down in France (compared to the standing theaters in China and Canada) to view a well-made film introduction to the people, cities, and natural wonders of France.

TOURING TIPS This pavilion is rich in atmosphere attributable to its detailed street scenes and bygone era flavor.

The streets of the French pavilion are diminutive and become quite congested when visitors line up for the film. Waits in line can be substantial here, so we recommend viewing before 11 A.M. and after 7 P.M.

Attractions in France include:

Impressions de France

Type of Show: Film essay on the French people and country

When to Go: Before 11 A.M. and after 7 P.M.

Authors' Rating: An exceedingly beautiful film; not to be missed; ★★★★

Overall Appeal by Age Group:

Pre-school	Grade School	Teens	Young Adults	Over 30	Senior Citizens
★★½	★★★½	★★★½	★★★★½	★★★★½	★★★★½

Duration of Presentation: Approximately 18 minutes
Pre-Show Entertainment: None
Probable Waiting Time: 12 minutes (at suggested times)

United Kingdom

DESCRIPTION AND COMMENTS   A variety of periods and facades, with attempts to create city, town, and rural atmospheres, are compressed into this pavilion, which is mostly shops. The Rose and Crown Pub and Dining Room is the only World Showcase restaurant with dining on the water side of the promenade. A city square, with classic formal facade, copies a look found in London and Edinburgh. One street has a 1500s style thatched-roof cottage, a four-story timber and plaster building, a pre-Georgian plaster building, a formal Palladian exterior of dressed stone, and a city square with Hyde Park bandstand (whew!).

TOURING TIPS   We would have to say that this was our least favorite pavilion—not bad, mind you—we just think it could have been a whole lot better. There are no attractions here to create congestion, so tour at any time you wish. Reservations are not needed to enjoy the Pub section of the Rose and Crown Pub, making it a nice place to stop for a beer along about mid-afternoon.

Canada

DESCRIPTION AND COMMENTS   The cultural, natural, and architectural diversity of the United States' neighbor to the north is reflected in this large and impressive pavilion. Thirty-foot totem poles embellish an Indian village situated beneath the gables of a magnificent château-style hotel. Near the hotel is a rugged stone building said to be modeled after a famous landmark near Niagara Falls, reflective of Canada's British influence. Canada also has a fine film extolling its many national, cultural, and natural virtues. Titled *O Canada!* the film is very enlightening, and demonstrates the immense pride Canadians have in their beautiful country. Visitors leave the theater through Victoria Gardens, inspired by the famed Butchart Gardens of British Columbia.

TOURING TIPS A large-capacity theater attraction which sees fairly heavy early morning attendance since it is the first pavilion encountered as one travels counter-clockwise around World Showcase Lagoon. We recommend late afternoon or early evening as the best time for viewing the film. Le Cellier, a restaurant serving cafeteria-style on the lower level of the Canadian pavilion, is the only non-fast-food restaurant in the World Showcase that does not require reservations.

Attractions in Canada include:

O Canada!

Type of Show: Film essay on the Canadian people and country

When to Go: Late afternoon or early evening

Special Comments: Audience stands during performance

Authors' Rating: Makes you want to catch the first plane to Canada! ★★★★½

Overall Appeal by Age Group:

Pre-school	Grade School	Teens	Young Adults	Over 30	Senior Citizens
★★½	★★★	★★★½	★★★★	★★★★½	★★★★½

Duration of Presentation: Approximately 18 minutes

Pre-Show Entertainment: None

Probable Waiting Time: 10 minutes

EPCOT Center Ride Information

—— *Cutting Down Your Time in Line by Understanding the Rides* ——

EPCOT Center has fewer rides overall than the Magic Kingdom (see "Cutting Down Your Time in Line by Understanding the Rides," Magic Kingdom, page 101). All of them are major features of the park and rank on a par with Pirates of the Caribbean and the Jungle Cruise in the Magic Kingdom in terms of scope, detail, imagination, and spectacle. All but one or two EPCOT Center rides are fast loading with large overall carrying capacities. Thus, EPCOT Center rides are, on average, well engineered and very efficient. Lines at EPCOT Center are often somewhat longer than in the Magic Kingdom, but usually move quickly. There are no amusement park rides at EPCOT Center and no rides which are specifically intended for children.

In the Magic Kingdom traffic flow is to some extent a function of the popularity and engineering of individual rides. At EPCOT Center traffic flow is much more affected by the way the park is laid out. In terms of touring efficiency it is important to understand how the Magic Kingdom rides operate. At EPCOT Center this knowledge is decidedly less important.

EPCOT Center
Theater Information

—— *Cutting Down Your Time in Line*
   by Understanding the Shows ——

By a show we are referring to a theater performance as opposed to a ride. EPCOT Center, unlike the Magic Kingdom, offers more theater presentations than rides. While not as complex from a crowd management perspective as many of the rides, a little enlightenment concerning the operation of the various theater attractions may save some valuable touring time.

Theater attractions at EPCOT Center operate in three distinct phases:

1. There is the audience, which is actually in the theater viewing the presentation.

2. There are the visitors who have passed through the turnstile into a holding area or waiting lobby. These people will be admitted to the theater as soon as the presentation currently in progress is concluded.

3. There is the outside line. Those waiting here will be admitted to the waiting lobby when there is room, and will ultimately move from the waiting lobby to the theater.

Most of the theaters at EPCOT Center hold a lot of people. Thus when a new audience is admitted to the theater the outside line (if there is one) will usually disappear. Except on extremely busy days the maximum wait for a given theater presentation should be no longer than twice the time of the performance itself.

Theater capacity and the popularity of the presentation, along with the level of attendance in the park, determine how long you will have to wait in line to see a particular show. For specific information concerning each theater attraction, see pages 139–64, which include descriptions of the respective presentations.

Live Entertainment in EPCOT Center

Live entertainment in EPCOT Center is somewhat more diversified, as might be expected, than that of the Magic Kingdom. World Showcase provides almost unlimited potential for representative entertainment from the respective nations, and Future World allows for a new wave of creativity in live entertainment offerings.

Some information concerning the live entertainment on the day of your visit can be obtained from the information desk in the Earth Station lobby. Our experience, however, indicates that the Earth Station attendants are not usually too well informed. Another source of information is the WorldKey Information Service. WorldKey usually has the answers, but it is not as direct as quizzing an attendant.

Listed below are some of the performers and performances you are likely to encounter.

Future World Brass	A roving brass band that marches and plays according to a more or less extemporaneous schedule near Spaceship Earth and at other Future World locations.
Disney Characters	Costumed characters who lurk in the CommuniCore area of Future World, playing with children and posing for pictures.
American Gardens Stage	The site of EPCOT Center's premier live performances is near *The American Adventure*, facing World Showcase Lagoon, in a large amphitheater. Top talent imported from all over the world plays the American Gardens Stage on a limited engagement basis. Many shows highlight the music, dance, and costumes of the performer's home country.
IllumiNations	An after-dark show, consisting of music,

fireworks, erupting fountains, special lighting, and laser technology performed on the World Showcase Lagoon when the park is open late.

Around World Showcase

A variety of unscheduled, impromptu performances take place in and around the various pavilions of World Showcase. You may encounter a strolling mariachi group in Mexico, street actors in Italy, a fife-and-drum corps or a singing group (The Voices of Liberty) at *The American Adventure*, traditional songs and dances in Japan, comical street musicians (the Pearly Kings and Queens) and a bagpipe band in England, white-faced mimes in France, and a versatile musical group, the Maple Leaf Brass, in Canada.

Dinner Shows

The restaurants in World Showcase, as well as the Odyssey Restaurant, serve up healthy portions of live entertainment to accompany the victuals. Examples of restaurant floorshow fare include folk dancers and a baskapelle band in Germany, singing waiters in Italy, and electronic music at the Odyssey. Restaurant shows are performed at both lunch and dinner seatings. Reservations are required (see "Eating in EPCOT Center," below) except at the Odyssey.

Skyleidoscope

A daytime mixed-media spectacle at the World Showcase Lagoon featuring speed boats, hang gliders, and small aircraft in a good vs. evil morality fantasy topped off with music and fireworks (right, we couldn't believe it either). Usually kicks off about 2 P.M.

Eating in EPCOT Center

Having reviewed the restaurants of EPCOT Center since the park opened in 1982, we have seen a lot of changes, most of them for the better. There is more variety now than ever before, and more choices for folks who do not want to take the time for a full-service, sit-down meal. The quality of fast food available is quite good, better than in the Magic Kingdom, and the newest addition to the full-service restaurants, the Akershus Restaurant in Norway, is exceptional in every respect.

Where certain World Showcase restaurants were once timid about delivering an honest representation of the host nation's cuisine, we are now seeing bold ethnic menus in Norway, *mole* in Mexico, and finally, sushi in Japan. Restaurants in Morocco, England, and China, however, still sacrifice ethnic authenticity to please the tastes of most Americans, who, more than anyone, need their palates challenged (or need not to be eating in ethnic restaurants).

Many EPCOT Center restaurants are overpriced, most conspicuously Alfredo's (Italy), Mitsukoshi (Japan), Nine Dragons (China), and the Coral Reef at The Living Seas Pavilion. Les Chefs and Le Bistro (France), Akershus (Norway), Biergarten (Germany), and San Angel Inn (Mexico) represent good value through a combination of well-prepared food, ambiance, and in the case of Germany, entertainment.

Making reservations for full-service restaurants still involves standing in line in the morning when you would rather be doing something else, and in most cases, abandoning your touring itinerary to hustle (usually from the opposite side of the park) to the restaurant to be seated. The restaurants are such an integral part of EPCOT Center, however, that we think it would be a mistake not to have a meal in at least one of them.

— *Getting a Handle on the World Showcase Restaurants* —

Getting a reservation for a particular restaurant depends on its popularity and seating capacity, and, of course, the size of the crowd on the day of your visit. Each restaurant has seatings for both lunch and dinner. Reservations must be made on the day of the meal.

To insure the restaurant and seating of your choice, arrive at the entrance turnstiles, passport in hand, 45 minutes before EPCOT Center opens. Upon admission go quickly to Earth Station (the building at the base of the dome). Both lunch and dinner reservations can be made at the same time. Be prepared with alternatives for both restaurants and seatings in case your first choices are filled. If there are several folks in your party, perhaps one might volunteer to make the restaurant reservations while the others ride Spaceship Earth. Spaceship Earth disembarks passengers into Earth Station, thus making it fairly easy to regroup.

If you don't follow this plan, you will have a long wait in line to make reservations with no guarantee that anything will be available. On many days the World Showcase restaurants book solid for preferred seating times within an hour to an hour and a half of the park opening. Even if you get a reservation, you will have spent your most productive/crowd-free touring time in the process.

If you follow one of our touring plans, you will be near the United States pavilion (The American Adventure) at noon. We suggest, therefore, a lunch reservation for noon or 12:30 P.M. at nearby Germany. For dinner, we recommend reservations at the San Angel Inn in Mexico or at the Akershus in Norway. If you plan to eat your evening meal at the Coral Reef, you may want to wait until after dinner to see the attraction itself, instead of seeing it early in the morning.

If you blow it and arrive late but still want to eat in one of the World Showcase restaurants, here are some strategies that often pay off:

1. Go to a WorldKey Information terminal *outside* of Earth Station (there are some located around the bridgeway connecting Future World to World Showcase) and use the system as described on page 137 to call up an attendant. Try to make a reservation.

2. If you can't get a reservation via WorldKey, go to the restaurant of your choice and apply at the door for a reservation. Sometimes

only lunch reservations are taken at the door, but lunch and dinner menus are comparable if not the same. Just have your main meal at lunch.

3. If neither of the foregoing work, go to the restaurant of your choice and ask the hostess to call you if she gets a cancellation. A reservation is held about 15–20 minutes before the vacancy is filled with "standby" diners. Very early and very late seatings have more "no-shows."

4. If the options mentioned above do not pan out, you can often get a table just by showing up at the Moroccan Restaurant (reservations often go unfilled owing to American unfamiliarity with the cuisine). If Moroccan is too adventurous for you, try Le Cellier, a cafeteria in the Canadian pavilion, or the Land Grille Room in The Land pavilion, which is often overlooked at dinner time.

—— *The Restaurants of EPCOT Center* ——

While eating at EPCOT Center can be a consummate hassle, it is likewise true that an afternoon in the World Showcase section of EPCOT Center without a dinner reservation is something like not having a date on the day of the prom. Each pavilion has a beautifully seductive ethnic eatery, offering the hungry tourist the gastronomic delights of the world. To tour one after another of these exotic foreign settings and not partake is almost beyond the limits of willpower.

In all honesty, the food in some of the World Showcase restaurants is not very compelling, but the overall experience is exhilarating. And if you fail to dine in the World Showcase, you will miss out on one of EPCOT Center's more delightful features.

In our opinion there is no logical correlation between price, quality, and popularity of the World Showcase restaurants. Our researchers, for example, found L'Originale Alfredo di Roma Ristorante (Italy) frequently disappointing in spite of the fact that it is almost always one of the first two restaurants to fill its seatings. To help you make your choice, a data summary of each World Showcase restaurant requiring reservations (plus the Canadian Le Cellier) is presented below. All full-service restaurants have children's menus.

Canada

Le Cellier (No Reservations Required)

This is the only cafeteria-style restaurant in the World Showcase and represents a tasty and economical choice for those who want a nicer meal but do not have reservations elsewhere.

Time to go: Lunch—before 11:30 and after 2:00

Dinner—before 5:30 and after 8:00

Entree Prices: Lunch, $6–$13   Dinner, $6–$13

United Kingdom

Rose & Crown Pub & Dining Room (Reservations Required)

Seating Capacity: 152

Popularity: More popular for lunch. About the fifth to book for dinner, owing more to its small size than to its popularity.

Critic's Rating: Hearty but nothing to get excited about.

Atmosphere: Excellent, warm pub interior with an unparalleled view of the World Showcase Lagoon.

Entree Prices: Lunch, $6–$8   Dinner, $9–$17

Entertainment: Madrigal music with lute.

Comments: Fish & chips, steak and kidney pie, roast beef and basic pub fare make up the menu here.

France

Les Chefs de France (Reservations Required)

Seating Capacity: 162

Popularity: Usually the third restaurant to fill its reservations.

Critic's Rating: Very good and sometimes excellent.

Atmosphere: Elegant and bright, but not intimate or romantic.

Entree Prices: Lunch, $5–$12   Dinner, $12–$19

Entertainment: None.

Comments: Les Chefs apply their art with great success to fresh Florida seafood.

Le Bistro de Paris (Reservations Required)

Seating Capacity: 150

Popularity: Very popular. Many patrons make reservations here by mistake, thinking they are scheduling for Les Chefs.

Critic's Rating: Good, but lacking the creativity and delicacy of Les Chefs.

Atmosphere: Bright and bustling.

Entree Prices: Lunch, $7–$11   Dinner, $12–$19

Entertainment: None.

Comments: A good choice for picky American "meat and potato" diners. Specializes in continental peasant fare.

Morocco

El Marrakech (Reservations Required)

Seating Capacity: 250

Popularity: Normally the seventh or eighth restaurant to fill its reservations.

Critic's Rating: Different, usually good; portions sometimes skimpy.

Atmosphere: Colorful and exotic.

Entree Prices: Lunch, $7–$11   Dinner, $12–$15

Entertainment: Belly dancing and a Moroccan band.

Comments: Interesting fare almost impossible to find except in the largest of U.S. cities. Because Moroccan food is so unknown to most visitors, El Marrakech sometimes has tables available for walk-ins.

Japan

Mitsukoshi Restaurant (Reservations Required)

Seating Capacity: Teppanyaki Dining, 160; Tempura Kiku, 27

Popularity: Normally the sixth or seventh restaurant to fill its reservations.

Critic's Rating: Nothing to write home about. Eschews the diverse and beautiful traditional Japanese fare for teppan table cooking a la the Benihana of Tokyo chain restaurants.

Atmosphere: Enchanting stained wood and paper walls; traditional Japanese surroundings.

Entree Prices: Lunch, $7–$11   Dinner, $12–$25

Entertainment: Provided by the chopping, juggling teppan chefs.

Comments: This restaurant has missed a wonderful opportunity to introduce authentic Japanese cuisine to the American public. If you go, we recommend the Tempura Kiku, a small section of the dining room specializing in tempura. Finally, be aware that diners at the teppan tables (large tables with a flattop grill in the middle) are seated at a common table with other parties.

Italy

L'Originale Alfredo di Roma Ristorante (Reservations Required)

Seating Capacity: 254

Popularity: Usually the first or second restaurant to fill its seating.

Critic's Rating: Overrated and somewhat overpriced. Our guess is that many diners feel more familiar with Italian food than with the other ethnic cuisines available at EPCOT Center, thus making Alfredo's popular beyond its ability to deliver.

Atmosphere: Elegant, bright, with beautiful murals adorning several walls.

Entree Prices: Lunch, $8–$11   Dinner, $10–$23

Entertainment: Wonderfully talented singing waiters and waitresses erupting in a profusion of song, including Italian traditional, classical, and opera.

Comments: If you go, try veal or chicken. If you must have pasta, order an appetizer portion or a side dish.

China

Nine Dragons (Reservations Required)

Seating Capacity: 200

Popularity: Usually the sixth or seventh restaurant to fill its reservations.

Atmosphere: Traditional Chinese.

Entree Prices: Lunch, $8–$12   Dinner, $9–$18.50

Comments: Menu items, preparations, and serving style make it almost impossible to eat family style as do the Chinese and as do most Americans in traditional Chinese restaurants. Instead, each diner gets a "big ol' platter all to his own self, like at the Ponderosa."

Germany

Biergarten (Reservations Required)

Seating Capacity: 360

Popularity: Usually the fifth or sixth to book its reservations.

Critic's Rating: Food is hearty. The dinner show is fun and rousing, and the overall atmosphere is festive.

Atmosphere: The largest of the reservation restaurants. Multiple tiers of diners surround a stage where yodelers, dancers, and a German band perform in the evening at each scheduled seating. The beer flows freely and diners join in the singing, making the Biergarten a happy, delightful place to dine.

Entree Prices: Lunch $6–$14   Dinner, $11–$17

Entertainment: Yodelers, dancers, singers, and a German band.

Comments: Best bets are the wursts and the spitted chicken. Because of the size of the Biergarten, it is an above-average bet for getting in without a reservation as a "standby."

Mexico

San Angel Inn Restaurante (Reservations Required)

Seating Capacity: 158

Popularity: Usually the third or fourth restaurant to fill its reservations.

Critic's Rating: Excellent food and excellent value.

Atmosphere: Superb, truly romantic. You sit beneath the stars in a re-creation of a small village on the banks of the Rio del Tiempo with the jungle and an Aztec pyramid in the background.

Entree Prices: Lunch, $7–$13   Dinner, $10–$20

Entertainment: None.

Comments: Delightful menu goes beyond the normal Mexican fare, offering regional and special dishes that are very difficult to find in the U.S. Our choice for the best all-around restaurant in EPCOT Center.

Norway

Akershus Restaurant

Seating Capacity: 200

Popularity: Steadily growing as the word spreads of its quality.

Critic's Rating: The most interesting menu in Walt Disney World.

Atmosphere: Scandinavian, bright and scrubbed, clean and cheery.

Entree Price (Buffet Only): Lunch, $4.25 (child) $8.50 (adult)

  Dinner, $6.50 (child) $13.25 (adult)

Entertainment: None.

Comments: A beautiful cold and hot buffet features salmon, herring, various Norwegian salads, and a variety of meats. Hearty, adventurous eating. Ranks right along with San Angel Inn in Mexico as the best of the World Showcase restaurants.

Future World Reservation Restaurants

Future World restaurants are primarily fast-food establishments. There are, however, two exceptions, and both are worthy competitors of the World Showcase ethnic restaurants in terms of food quality, atmosphere, and menu creativity. What's more, they are sometimes forgotten in the great morning reservations rush.

The Land Pavilion

The Land Grille Room (Reservations Required)

Seating Capacity: 232

Popularity: Most popular at lunch. Often overlooked for dinner.

Critic's Rating: Good food and creative menu. A good choice for finicky eaters and beef-and-potato lovers.

Atmosphere: Elegant revolving platform which overlooks rain forest, prairie, and farm scenes along the Listen to the Land boat-ride route. Unexpectedly intimate and romantic.

Entree Prices: Breakfast, $5–$10   Lunch, $6–$9   Dinner, $12–$20

Entertainment: None.

Comments: A nice change of pace. The only full-service restaurant in EPCOT Center that serves breakfast.

Living Seas Pavilion

Coral Reef Restaurant (Reservations Required)

Seating Capacity: 250

Popularity: Popular because of its novelty and fresh seafood specialty. Often the first to fill its reservations.

Critic's Rating: Does not live up to expectations.

Atmosphere: Diners eat fresh seafood and are surrounded by even fresher (live) seafood. Very interesting.

Entree Prices: Lunch, $10–$22   Dinner, $16–$24

Entertainment: Live fish viewing.

Comments: Great view, but the food is average and way overpriced. Go to the attractions to view fish and to one of Orlando's good local seafood restaurants to eat them.

Alternatives and Suggestions for Eating in EPCOT Center

Listed below are some suggestions for any dauntless, epicurean adventurer who is determined to eat at EPCOT Center:

1. Do not stand in lines at restaurants unless absolutely necessary. Use the WorldKey terminals (calling up an attendant) to make your reservations.

2. For fast-food meals, EPCOT Center is like the Magic Kingdom; eat before 11 A.M. or after 2 P.M. The Odyssey Restaurant and the Liberty Inn at the United States pavilion move people through pretty speedily, and sometimes you can get served in a reasonable time in The Land pavilion (the latter being a bit more iffy). Some of the food at The Land is a cut above the average; as for the other fast-food places mentioned, expect bulk.

3. Review the "Alternatives and Suggestions for Eating in the Magic Kingdom," page 110. Many tips for the Magic Kingdom also apply to EPCOT Center.

Shopping in EPCOT Center

The shops in Future World seem a little out of place, the atmosphere being too visionary and grandiose to accommodate the pettiness of the bargain table. Similarly, it obviously has been difficult to find merchandise consistent with the surroundings. Expressed differently, what is available for purchase in Future World is also available at a lot of other places (EPCOT and Disney trademark souvenirs being the exception).

The World Showcase shops add a lot of realism and atmosphere to the street scenes of which they are part. But it's the same high-priced merchandise which, for the most part, could be found on the shelves of better boutiques, import shops, and department stores almost anywhere in the nation.

EPCOT Center
One-Day Touring Plans

The EPCOT Center One-Day Touring Plans are field-tested, step-by-step itineraries for seeing all of the major attractions at EPCOT Center in one day with a minimum of waiting in line. They are designed to keep you ahead of the crowds while the park is filling in the morning and to place you at the less crowded attractions during EPCOT Center's busier hours of the day. They assume that you would be happier doing a *little* extra walking as opposed to a lot of extra standing in line.

Touring EPCOT Center in one day is much more strenuous and demanding than touring the Magic Kingdom in a single day. To begin with, EPCOT Center is about twice as large as the Magic Kingdom. Secondly, and unlike the Magic Kingdom, EPCOT Center has essentially no effective in-park transportation system; wherever you want to go, it's always quicker and easier to walk. Where visitors arriving at the Magic Kingdom disperse rather evenly, visitors arriving at EPCOT Center tend to cluster. Spaceship Earth forms immense lines ten minutes after opening, while the rest of the park is virtually empty. The One-Day Touring Plans will assist you in avoiding crowds and bottlenecks on days of moderate to heavy attendance, but cannot lessen the distance you will have to walk. Wear comfortable shoes and be prepared for a lot of hiking. On days of lighter attendance, when crowd conditions are not a critical factor, the Touring Plans will serve primarily to help you organize your tour.

On days of moderate to heavy attendance follow the Touring Plans exactly; do not deviate from them except:

1. When you do not want to experience an attraction called for on the Touring Plans—if an attraction is listed that does not interest you, simply skip that step and proceed to the next step.

2. When you encounter an extremely long line at an attraction called for by the Touring Plans—the central idea is to avoid crowds, not to

join them. Crowds build and dissipate throughout the day for a variety of reasons. The Touring Plans anticipate most normally recurring crowd-flow patterns but cannot predict spontaneously arising situations (Spaceship Earth breaking down, for instance, with the hundreds of people standing in line suddenly descending on the nearby Universe of Energy). If the line is ridiculously long, simply skip that step and move on to the next, coming back later for another try.

Two outline versions of One-Day Touring Plans follow this section; each is tailored for groups with different needs.

Traffic Patterns in EPCOT Center

After admiring for many years the way traffic is engineered at the Magic Kingdom, we were somewhat amazed at the way EPCOT Center was laid out. At the Magic Kingdom, Main Street, U.S.A., with its many shops and eateries, serves as a huge gathering place when the park opens and subsequently funnels visitors to the central hub; from there, equally accessible entrances branch off to the various lands. Thus the crowds are first welcomed and entertained (on Main Street) and then distributed almost equally to the respective lands.

At EPCOT Center, by contrast, Spaceship Earth, the park's premier architectural landmark and one of its featured attractions, is situated just inside the main entrance. When visitors enter the park they invariably and almost irresistibly head right for it. Hence crowds tend to bottleneck as soon as the park opens less than seventy-five yards from the admission turnstiles. For those in the know, however, the congestion at Spaceship Earth provides some excellent opportunities for escaping waits at other rides and shows in the Future World section of EPCOT Center. If you are one of the first in the gate do not hesitate to experience Spaceship Earth (you will probably not find a shorter line later). If Spaceship Earth lines wind around the side of adjoining Earth Station, pass by the ride.

Early-morning crowds are contained in the Future World half of EPCOT Center for the simple reason that most of the rides and shows are located in Future World. Distribution of visitors to the various Future World attractions, except Spaceship Earth, is fairly equal. Many of the early visitors to CommuniCore West and the attractions located behind it arrive by accident while trying to find the end of the line to Spaceship Earth. Morning visitors trying to move counter to the main traffic flow would bypass Spaceship Earth (unless the line was short) and proceed directly to The Living Seas, then to The Land, and from there to Journey into Imagination.

When World Showcase, the other main section of EPCOT Center, opens (usually at 10 A.M.), most early visitors are still touring Future World. Thus the opening of World Showcase does not have a dramatic effect on the distribution of visitors to the overall park. Or expressed differently, between 9 A.M. and 11 A.M., there are more people entering Future World via the entrance than departing Future World into World Showcase. Attendance continues building in Future World until sometime between noon and 2 P.M. World Showcase attendance builds rapidly with the approach of the midday meal. Exhibits at the far end of World Showcase Lagoon report playing to full-capacity audiences from about noon on through 6:30 P.M.–7:30 P.M.

The central focus of World Showcase in the eyes of most visitors is its atmosphere, featuring international landmarks, romantic street scenes, quaint shops, and ethnic restaurants. Unlike the Magic Kingdom with its premier rides and attractions situated along the far perimeters of its respective lands, World Showcase has only two major entertainment draws (Maelstrom in Norway, and *The American Adventure*). Thus, where the Magic Kingdom uses its super attractions to draw and distribute the crowds rather evenly, EPCOT Center's cluster of premier attractions in Future World serves to hold the greater part of the crowd in the smaller part of the park. With the exception of making restaurant reservations, therefore, there is no compelling reason to rush to the World Showcase section of the park. The bottom line in Future World is a crowd that builds all morning and into the early afternoon. The two main sections of EPCOT Center do not approach equality in attendance until the approach of the evening meal. It should be stated, however, that evening crowds in World Showcase do not compare with the size of morning and midday crowds in Future World. Attendance throughout EPCOT Center is normally lighter in the evening.

An interesting observation at EPCOT Center from a crowd-distribution perspective is the indifference of repeat visitors relative to favoring one attraction over another. At the Magic Kingdom repeat visitors make a mad dash for their favorite ride and their preferences are strong and well defined. At EPCOT Center, by contrast, many returning tourists indicate that (with the possible exceptions of Spaceship Earth and *The American Adventure*) they enjoy the major rides and features "about the same." The conclusion suggested here is that touring patterns at EPCOT Center will be more systematic and predictable (i.e., by the numbers, clockwise, counterclockwise, etc.) than at the Magic Kingdom.

Closing time at EPCOT Center does not precipitate congestion similar to that observed when the Magic Kingdom closes. One primary reason for the ease of departure from EPCOT Center is that its parking lot is adjacent to the park as opposed to being separated by a lake as in the Magic Kingdom. At the Magic Kingdom, departing visitors bottleneck at the monorail to the Transportation and Ticket Center and main parking lot. At EPCOT Center you can proceed directly to your car.

—— EPCOT Center One-Day Touring Plan for Adults ——

FOR: **Adults without small children**.
ASSUMES: Willingness to experience all major rides and shows.

DIRECTION	EXPLANATION
1. Have your admission paid and be at the turnstile ready to go forty-five minutes before the park's stated opening time. NOTE: EPCOT Center often opens a half hour before its stated opening time.	Being one of the first visitors admitted to the park will allow you to see many of the most popular attractions at the time of day when the lines are shortest. The thirty to forty-five minutes you invest in your early morning arrival will literally save you hours during the remainder of your touring day.
2. When you are admitted to the park proceed posthaste to Spaceship Earth (the huge geodesic dome just inside the entrance). If your top priority is obtaining reservations for a World Showcase lunch or dinner, skip Spaceship Earth until late afternoon and proceed directly to Step 3. If you want to have your cake and eat it too, find someone in your party who will volunteer to forego Spaceship Earth and have him run ahead to make meal reservations while you take the ride. He can meet you inside Earth Station where the ride disembarks.	Spaceship Earth, because of its theme, distinctive design, and positioning near the entrance to the park, develops an incredible line mere minutes after EPCOT Center opens. Moreover, because of the attraction's popularity, the line remains quite long all day. The only shot you have, therefore, of avoiding a 45-minute or longer wait for Spaceship Earth is to hop in line during the first few minutes that the park is open. A short line for Spaceship Earth (30-minute wait) is one which fills the attraction's queue area (the system of parallel railings situated in front of Spaceship Earth). A medium line would

DIRECTION	EXPLANATION

Another tactic is to send one person in your group to make meal reservations while the others get in line for Spaceship Earth. As long as those standing in line do not progress into the queue area immediately in front of the ride (divided by parallel railings), it will be relatively easy for the person making the meal reservations to join the rest of the party in line. If the reservations maker has not arrived by the time those waiting for the ride have progressed to the parallel railings area, they can simply stay put, allowing other parties to pass them until the reservations maker arrives.

completely fill the queue area and would additionally extend down the sidewalk to the right (west side) of Earth Station. A medium line usually corresponds to a wait of 35 to 55 minutes. A long line for Spaceship Earth extends past Earth Station and into the open area between CommuniCore East and West. Waiting time for a long line is from one to three hours. If the line you encounter is short to mid-medium, go ahead and see Spaceship Earth. *If the line is longer, bypass Spaceship Earth for the time being.*

3. Go directly to a WorldKey Information video display terminal and make restaurant reservations for lunch and dinner. We recommend asking for a late seating for dinner (8 P.M.–9 P.M.). This will allow maximum touring flexibility in the itinerary and take advantage of the fact that World Showcase usually stays open later than Future World. If your tummy throws a fit, grab a snack around 5 P.M. to tide you over.

If you follow one of our touring plans you will be in the vicinity of the United States pavilion (The American Adventure) at noon. We suggest, therefore, a lunch reservation for noon or 12:30 P.M.

The better restaurants at EPCOT Center are sit-down restaurants requiring reservations which must be made on the same day that you plan to dine. For greater elaboration see "Eating in EPCOT Center," page 169, and the special section on the WorldKey Information Service, page 137. If you have only one day to visit the EPCOT Center, you may be better off making a reservation for dinner only and having a fast-food lunch.

DIRECTION	EXPLANATION

at Germany. For dinner, we recommend reservations at Mexico or Norway, but the two French restaurants are also good.

4. Go directly to The Living Seas and enjoy.

This is a new and popular attraction, and the best time to catch it is in the morning.

5. Go directly to The Land, situated behind CommuniCore West and take the boat trip, Listen to the Land.

The Land pavilion consists of three attractions and a variety of restaurants. The best way to see this attraction is to arrive early before the restaurant crowd hits. On a One-Day Touring Plan we bypass for the time being the other two attractions here.

6. Proceed to Journey into Imagination, the next big pavilion to the right of The Land. Ride Journey into Imagination first, then see the 3-D film, *Captain EO*, at the Magic Eye Theater.

Following this Touring Plan, you should arrive at Journey into Imagination before attendance gets particularly heavy. Ride first and then see the movie for most efficient crowd avoidance.

With the popularity of *Captain EO*, it may be better to see the flick first and then enjoy the ride. The direct entrance to *Captain EO* is around to the far left of the Journey into Imagination pavilion. If you choose to take the ride first you can proceed to *Captain EO* by taking the corridor to your right after you get off the ride.

7. Exit Future World and proceed directly to World Showcase.

By this time crowds will be building throughout the Future World section of the park. Leave

DIRECTION	EXPLANATION
	Future World and proceed to World Showcase where crowds will not as yet have reached their peak.
8. Bypassing Canada and England for the time being, go directly to France and see the film *Impressions de France*.	By moving directly to the far end of World Showcase Lagoon you can reach the French and American exhibits before they become extremely crowded. The French exhibit, particularly, becomes quite congested as the noon hour approaches.
9. Go directly to the American pavilion and see *The American Adventure*.	This is a large-capacity theater production which will accommodate large numbers of viewers even when the park is busy.
10. If the lines are not prohibitive (and if you did not make reservations for a sit-down lunch) grab a bite to eat at the Liberty Inn, or quicker yet, at the bratwurst stand on the left side of Germany.	With the exception of some street vendors, this is the only source of fast-food meals in the immediate area. Liberty Inn is quite large and can probably serve more food to more people in less time than any other restaurant in World Showcase. If you are not hungry, stop later for a bratwurst from the street vendor in Germany.
11. Whether you eat or not, go next to the Japanese exhibit and from there proceed in a counterclockwise direction to Italy, Germany, and the People's Republic of China. At the Chinese exhibit, see the film *Wonders of China*.	The entire park will be very busy by this time of day. Enjoy the atmosphere of the respective international pavilions.

DIRECTION	EXPLANATION
12. Bypass Mexico for the time being and reenter Future World; see the World of Motion.	This is a continuously loading ride where the wait in line is almost always tolerable.
13. Go next door and tour Horizons.	This is a continuously loading ride where the line is almost always tolerable except when the audience of a just-concluded Universe of Energy performance (next pavilion in the direction of the dome) descends en masse. If you encounter long lines at Horizons any time during the evening, just take a break; they will usually work themselves out in about 10–15 minutes.
14. Next, go to the Universe of Energy and ask an attendant what the anticipated wait will be. If less than 45 minutes, stay and see the show, otherwise, proceed to Step 15.	Lines at the Universe of Energy vary considerably in length (owing in part to the unreliable nature of nearby Spaceship Earth, which breaks down occasionally, dispersing its masses of waiting people primarily to Universe of Energy). If you catch Universe of Energy at a bad time, skip it for the present and try again later. If you can get in in less than 45 minutes, bite the bullet and hop in line.
15. Cross through Communi-Core and return to The Land. See the film *Symbiosis* at the Harvest Theater and a performance of *Kitchen Kabaret*.	The lunch crowd will be gone by the time you return to The Land. See whichever of the two productions begins sooner, followed by the other. This is a good time and place to grab a snack if your dinner reservation is for a late seating as recommended.

DIRECTION	EXPLANATION
16. While in Future World, see Spaceship Earth and/or Universe of Energy if you missed them earlier.	Spaceship Earth will have its shortest lines between 5:30 P.M. and 7:30 P.M. (which only means that the lines will be comparatively short; expect at least a forty-five minute wait). Lines at the Universe of Energy should be tolerable unless some other nearby attraction is not operating.
17. Backtrack to the World Showcase and see England followed by Canada; at Canada see the film *O Canada!*	Be sure to see England first and then Canada.
18. An hour or so before your dinner seating go to Mexico and ride El Rio del Tiempo, the River of Time.	This ride has long lines until after 6 P.M. on most days.
19. Walk next door to Norway and ride Maelstrom, the adventure boat ride, and then proceed to your dinner reservation (try either Mexico or Norway).	
20. After dinner, if you have any time or energy left, visit or revisit the EPCOT Center attractions of your choice.	

NOTE: EPCOT Center One-Day Touring Plan for Adults operates under the assumption that you are willing to do some extra walking to avoid long waits in line. There is, therefore, some backtracking involved. If you follow the Touring Plan and move quickly from Steps 1 through 9, particularly, you will normally be able to see almost the entire park in a single day at an acceptable pace and minimal waits in line.

— Outline of EPCOT Center One-Day Touring Plan, for Adults —

1. Pay your admission and be waiting at the turnstiles forty-five minutes before the park's stated opening time. Remember, sometimes EPCOT Center opens a half hour before its stated opening time. Therefore, if the stated opening time is 9 A.M., be there and ready to go at 8:15 A.M.

2. Go quickly and directly to Spaceship Earth—if the lines are short to mid-medium (see Step 2 in the elaborated version), go ahead and ride; if the lines exceed acceptable length, bypass until the evening hours. If restaurant reservations are a top priority, skip Spaceship Earth and go directly to Step 3.

3. Use the WorldKey Information terminals in the Earth Station lobby to make meal reservations. Try to get a late (8 P.M.– 9 P.M.) seating.

4. Go directly to The Living Seas and enjoy.

5. Proceed directly to The Land—take the boat trip Listen to the Land.

6. Go next to Journey into Imagination—ride Journey into Imagination; in the same pavilion view the 3-D movie at the Magic Eye Theater.

7. Go back through CommuniCore West (without stopping) and depart the Future World section of the park.

8. Bypass Canada and England for the moment; go directly to France and see *Impressions de France*.

9. Go past Japan for the time being to the American pavilion—see *The American Adventure*.

10. Eat lunch at the Liberty Inn if you are hungry and if the lines are not too long. If the lines are long, try the bratwurst stand to the left of Germany.

11. Backtrack to tour the Japanese exhibit. From there proceed counterclockwise to tour Italy, Germany, and China; at China see the movie *Wonders of China*.

12. Bypass Mexico and reenter Future World—see the World of Motion.

13. Go to Horizons. If the line is long, take a 15-minute break and then return.
14. Go to the Universe of Energy—if the wait is less than forty-five minutes, stay for the show; otherwise proceed to Step 15.
15. Cross through CommuniCore and return to The Land—while there see *Kitchen Kabaret* and, at the Harvest Theater, see *Symbiosis*. Grab a snack if you have reservations for a late dinner seating.
16. In Future World, see Spaceship Earth and/or the Universe of Energy if you missed them earlier.
17. Backtrack to the World Showcase—go first to England and then to Canada; at Canada see *O Canada!*
18. An hour or so before your dinner seating go to Mexico and ride El Rio del Tiempo.
19. Go next door to Norway and ride Maelstrom, the boat ride, and then proceed to dinner.
20. If the park is still open after dinner, visit or revisit the EPCOT Center attractions of your choice.

What You Missed

Nothing is missed on this EPCOT Center One-Day Touring Plan except for Backstage Magic in CommuniCore, and various live entertainments and special events which differ from day to day. Shops and stationary exhibits in both sections of the park, however, are accorded less priority on the Touring Plan than are films and rides, and some visitors may wish to substitute expanded time at the shops and exhibits for some of the other attractions.

Outline of EPCOT Center One-Day Touring Plan, for Parents with Small Children

FOR: **Adults with children under eight years of age**.
ASSUMES: Periodic stops for rest, restrooms, and refreshment.

EPCOT Center is educationally oriented and considerably more adult in tone and presentation than is the Magic Kingdom. Most younger children enjoy EPCOT Center if their visit is seven hours or less in duration, and if their tour emphasizes the Future World section of the park. Younger children, especially grade school children, find the international atmosphere of the World Showcase exciting, but do not have the patience for much more than a quick walk-through. And while we found touring objectives of adults and younger children basically compatible in Future World, we noted that children tired quickly of World Showcase movies and shows (except for El Rio del Tiempo and Maelstrom) and tried to hurry their adult companions.

This EPCOT Center One-Day Touring Plan is designed to keep smaller children interested and happy without pushing them beyond the limits of their endurance. It is not a comprehensive touring plan, but attempts to balance a representative sampling of both sections of the park with the different interests and energy levels of children and adults.

1. Pay your admission and be waiting at the turnstiles forty-five minutes before the park opens. Remember, sometimes EPCOT Center opens a half hour before its stated opening time. If the stated opening time is 9 A.M., therefore, be on site and ready to go at 8:15 A.M.

2. Go quickly and directly to Spaceship Earth. If the lines are short to mid-medium (see Step 2 in the elaborated version), go ahead and ride; if the lines exceed acceptable length, bypass until later.

3. Stop at the Guest Relations desk in Earth Station (at the rear of Spaceship Earth) and obtain a schedule of live entertainment and special events for the day. Many of these offerings are

particularly appealing to children and can be worked into the Touring Plan at your discretion.

4. Go directly to The Living Seas and enjoy.

5. Proceed directly to The Land—take the boat trip Listen to the Land.

6. Go next to Journey into Imagination—ride Journey into Imagination; in the same pavilion view the 3-D movie at the Magic Eye Theater and visit The Image Works.

7. Depart Future World via CommuniCore West (without stopping) and go to Mexico in World Showcase. Ride El Rio del Tiempo.

8. Go next door to Norway and ride Maelstrom.

9. Proceed around the World Showcase Lagoon en route to *The American Adventure*, taking abbreviated tours of China, Germany, and Italy along the way. See *The American Adventure*.

10. Eat lunch at the Liberty Inn if you are hungry and if the lines are not too long. If the lines are long, obtain a snack from a sidewalk vendor and postpone lunch until you return to Future World.

11. Continue around World Showcase Lagoon stopping for quick visits at Japan, France, England, and Canada. At Canada see *O Canada!*

12. Reenter Future World—see the World of Motion.

13. Go to Horizons. If the line is long, take a 15-minute break and then return.

14. Go to the Universe of Energy—if the wait is less than forty-five minutes, stay for the show; otherwise proceed to Step 15.

15. Cross through CommuniCore and return to The Land—while there see *Kitchen Kabaret* and, at the Harvest Theater, see *Symbiosis*. Grab something to eat if you missed lunch earlier.

16. If you missed Spaceship Earth and/or the Universe of Energy, try them now.

17. Visit or revisit EPCOT Center attractions of your choice if you still have time and energy.

—— *Not to be Missed at EPCOT Center* ——

World Showcase	*The American Adventure*
	Maelstrom
Future World	Spaceship Earth
	Listen to the Land
	Journey into Imagination
	Captain EO
	It's Fun to Be Free
	Universe of Energy
	The Living Seas

EPCOT Center Summary

P.O. Box 1000, Lake Buena Vista, FL 32830-1000
Call ahead for opening/closing times
Type: Futuristic and International Theme Park   Phone (407) 824-4321

Admissions

Ticket options	Discounts	
One-Day Ticket	Children (3–9)	**yes**
3-Day World Passport	Children under 3	**free**
4-Day World Passport	Students	**varies**
5-Day World Passport	Military	**varies**
1-Year World Passport	Senior citizens	**varies**
	Group rates	**yes**

Credit cards accepted for admission: **MasterCard, American Express** and **VISA**.
Features included: **All**

Overall Appeal*

By age groups	Preschool	Grade School[1]	Teens	Young Adults	Over 30	Senior Citizens
	★★★	★★★½	★★★★	★★★★★	★★★★★	★★★★★

Touring Tips

Touring time
  Average: **Full day**
  Minimum: **Full day**
Touring strategy: **See narrative**
Rainy day touring: **Recommended**

Periods of lightest attendance
  Time of day: **Early morning, late evening**
Days: **Friday, Sunday**
  Times of year: **After Thanksgiving until 18th of December**

What the Critics Say

Rating of major features:
  See pages 139–78

Rating of functional and operational areas

Parking	★★★★★
Restrooms	★★★★★
Resting places	★★★★★
Crowd management	★★★★★
Aesthetic appeal of grounds	★★★★★
Cleanliness/maintenance	★★★★★

Services and Facilities

Restaurant/snack bar **Yes**	Lockers **Yes**
Vending machines (food/pop) **No**	Pet kennels **Yes**
Alcoholic beverages **Yes**	Gift shops **Yes**
Handicapped access **Yes**	Film sales **Yes**
Wheelchairs **Rental**	Rain check **No**
Baby strollers **Rental**	Private guided group tours **Yes**

---

[1] Appreciation dependent on maturity of child
* Critical ratings are based on a scale of zero to five stars with five stars being the best possible rating.

PART FIVE—The Disney-MGM Studios and Studio Tour

And Now for Something Completely Different (again)

Several years ago, the Disney folks decided they wanted to make movies for adults. Figuring that Snow White wouldn't share the set with Bette Midler mouthing four-letter words, they cranked up a brand new production company to handle the adult stuff. Results have been impressive; a complete rejuvenation with new faces and tremendous creativeness, and an amazing resurgence at the box office.

So, as a new era of Disney film and television success begins to crest, what better way to showcase and promote their product than with an all-new motion-picture and television entertainment park at Walt Disney World? The highly successful Universal Studios tour in southern California has demonstrated the public's voracious appetite for peeking "behind the scenes." The new Disney attraction will undoubtedly both satisfy this craving and sell a lot of movie tickets. Smart business.

The MGM Connection

To broaden the appeal and to lend additional historic impact, Disney has obtained the rights to use the MGM (Metro-Goldwyn-Mayer) name, the MGM film library, MGM motion picture and television titles, excerpts, costumes, music, sets, and even Leo, the MGM logo lion. Probably the two most readily recognized names in the motion picture industry, Disney and MGM in combination showcase more than 60 years of movie history.

Comparing Disney-MGM Studios to the Magic Kingdom and EPCOT Center

Such a comparison appears to be an "apples and oranges" proposition at first glance. The Magic Kingdom has modeled most of its attractions from Disney movie and TV themes; EPCOT Center has pioneered attractions and rides as vehicles for learning. Looking more closely, however, there are numerous similarities. Like EPCOT Center, the Disney-MGM Studios is at once fun and educational, and as in the Magic Kingdom, the themes for the various rides and shows are drawn from movies and television. All three parks rely heavily on Disney special effects and AudioAnimatronics (robotics) in their entertainment mix.

The Disney-MGM Studios is about the same size as the Magic Kingdom and about one-half as large as the sprawling EPCOT Center. Unlike the other parks, however, Disney-MGM Studios is a working motion picture and television production facility. This means, among other things, that more than half of the entire Studios area will be controlled access, with guests permitted only on tours and accompanied by guides, or restricted to observation walkways.

When EPCOT Center opened in 1982, Disney patrons expected a futuristic version of the Magic Kingdom. What they got was humanistic inspiration and a creative educational experience. Since then, the Disney folks have tried to inject a little more magic, excitement, and surprise into EPCOT Center. But remembering the occasional disappointment of those early EPCOT Center guests, Disney planners have fortified the Disney-MGM Studios with megadoses of action, suspense, surprise, and, of course, special effects. If you are interested in the history and technology of the motion picture and television industries, there is plenty of education to be had. However, if you feel lazy and just want to be entertained, the Disney-MGM Studios is a pretty good place to be.

—— *How Much Time To Allocate* ——

A guest really has to scurry to see all of EPCOT Center or the Magic Kingdom (some say it can't be done) in one day. The Disney-MGM Studios are more manageable. There is less walking and much less ground to cover by foot. Trams transport guests throughout much of the backlot and working areas, and the attractions in the open-access parts are concentrated in an area about the size of Main Street and Tomorrowland put together. There will be a day, no doubt, as the Disney-MGM Studios develops and grows, when you will need more than a day to see everything without hurrying. For the time being, however, the Studios are a nice one-day outing.

Because it is smaller, however, the Disney-MGM Studios is more affected by large crowds. Likewise, being the newest Disney theme park, large crowds can be considered the norm for the foreseeable future. To help you avoid the crowds we have developed **Touring Plans** for the Disney-MGM Studios which will keep you a step ahead of the mob and minimize any waits in line. Even when the park is heavily attended, however, you can see most everything in a day.

—— *Arriving and Getting Oriented* ——

The Disney-MGM Studios has its own pay parking lot and is also serviced by shuttle bus from the Transportation and Ticket Center, from EPCOT Center, and from Walt Disney World hotels. In addition, many of the larger "out-of-the-World" hotels shuttle guests to the Studios. If you drive, Walt Disney World's ubiquitous trams will arrive to transport you to the ticketing area and entrance gate.

As you enter, Guest Relations will be on your left, serving as a park headquarters and information center similar to City Hall in the Magic Kingdom and Earth Station at EPCOT Center. Check here for a schedule of live performances, lost persons, lost objects, emergencies, and general information. If you have not been provided with a map of the Studios, pick one up here. To the right of the entrance you will find lockers, strollers, and wheelchair rentals.

For the sake of orientation, about one-third of the entire complex is set up as a theme park. As at the Magic Kingdom you enter the park and pass down a main street; only this time it's Hollywood Boulevard of the 1920s and 30s. At the end of Hollywood Boulevard is a replica of Hollywood's long-famous Chinese Theater. While not as imposing as Cinderella Castle or EPCOT Center's Spaceship Earth, the Theater is nevertheless Disney-MGM Studios' focal landmark and serves as a good spot to meet if your group gets separated.

The open-access (theme park) section of the Studios is situated at the theater end of Hollywood Boulevard and around a lake off to the left of the Boulevard as you face the theater. Attractions in this section of the Studios are rides and shows, which you can experience according to your own tastes and timetable. The remainder of the Disney-MGM Studios consists of the working sound stages, technical facilities, wardrobe shops, administrative offices, animation studios, and backlot sets, which are accessible to visitors via a walking and tram Studio Tour.

—— *What To See* ——

As in our coverage of the Magic Kingdom and EPCOT Center, we have identified certain attractions as "not to be missed." We suggest, however, that you try everything. Usually exceeding your expectations, and always surprising, Disney rides and shows are rarely what you would anticipate.

Open-Access/Movie Theme Park

Hollywood Boulevard

Hollywood Boulevard is a palm-lined re-creation of Hollywood's main drag during the city's golden age. Architecture is streamlined *moderne* with art deco embellishments. Most of the theme park's service facilities are located here, interspersed with numerous shops and eateries. Shoppers can select from among Hollywood and movie-related souvenir items to one-of-a-kind collectibles obtained from studio auctions and estate sales. Disney trademark items are, of course, also available.

In addition to the services and commercial ventures, trolleys transport guests who want a lift from the park entrance to the Chinese Theater at the end of the Boulevard, and characters from Hollywood's heyday, as well as roving performers, entertain passers-by. The Boulevard also serves as the site for daily parades and other happenings.

Hollywood Boulevard is where both the entrance and the exit are located. Like Main Street in the Magic Kingdom, Hollywood Boulevard opens a half hour to an hour before the rest of the park, and closes a half hour to an hour after the rest of the park.

Hollywood Boulevard Services

Most of the park's service facilities are housed along Hollywood Boulevard, including the following:

Wheelchair & stroller rental	To the right of the entrance at Oscar's Super Service
Banking services/ Currency exchange	Sun Bank in the Guest Relations complex to the left of the entrance
Storage lockers	Rental lockers are located to the right of the main entrance on Hollywood Boulevard.

The Great Movie Ride

Type of Attraction: Disney mixed-media adventure ride

When to Go: Before 10:30 A.M. and after 3 P.M.

Special Comments: Possibly Disney's most spectacular ride to date; not to be missed

Authors' Rating: ★★★★★

Authors' Estimated Appeal By Age Group:

Pre-school	Grade School	Teens	Young Adults	Over 30	Senior Citizens
★★★★★	★★★★★	★★★★★	★★★★★	★★★★★	★★★★★

Duration of Ride: About 19 minutes

Average Wait in Line per 100 People Ahead of You: 2 minutes

Assumes: Normal staffing

Loading Speed: Fast

DESCRIPTION AND COMMENTS   Entering through a re-creation of Hollywood's Chinese Theater, guests board vehicles for a fast-paced tour through sound stage sets from such classic films as *Casablanca*, *The Wizard of Oz*, *Aliens*, *Raiders of the Lost Ark*, and many more. Each set is populated with new-generation Disney AudioAnimatronics (robots) as well as an occasional real human, all assisted by a variety of dazzling special effects. Disney's largest and most ambitious ride-through attraction, The Great Movie Ride encompasses 95,000 square feet and showcases some of the most famous scenes in filmmaking history. Life-sized AudioAnimatronic sculptures of stars such as Gene Kelly, John Wayne, James Cagney, Julie Andrews, and Harrison Ford inhabit the largest sets ever constructed for a Disney ride.

TOURING TIPS   The Great Movie Ride is a continuous-loading, high-capacity ride. Even when the lines are long they will disappear quickly. For shorter waits, however, ride in the early morning or during the late afternoon or evening.

Disney Television Theater

Type of Attraction: Audience participation television production

When to Go: Between 11 A.M. and 4 P.M.

Authors' Rating: Well-conceived, not to be missed; ★★★★½

Authors' Estimated Appeal by Age Group:

Pre-school	Grade School	Teens	Young Adults	Over 30	Senior Citizens
★★★	★★★★★	★★★★★	★★★★½	★★★★½	★★★★½

Duration of Presentation: About 30 minutes

Pre-Show Entertainment: Yes; participants are selected from the audience.

Probable Waiting Time: 10–15 minutes

DESCRIPTION AND COMMENTS   Audience volunteers come forward to participate in a television production where special effects are used to integrate the actions of the amateurs with footage of well-known TV stars. The combined result, a sort of video collage where the volunteers miraculously end up in the footage with the stars, is broadcast on large-screen monitors above the set. The outcome, always rated in yuks, depends on how the volunteers respond to their dramatic debuts. Of course, there are sneaky surprises to bring out the funniest in each of them.

TOURING TIPS   The theater seats 1,000 persons, so it is not usually difficult to get in.

Star Tours (opens 1990)

Type of Attraction: Space flight simulation ride

When to Go: In 1990 if you are patient; at Disneyland in California now, if you are not.

Special Comments: Expectant mothers are advised against riding.

Authors' Rating: Disney's absolute best, any time, any place; not to be missed; ★★★★★

Overall Appeal by Age Group (based on Disneyland survey):

Pre-school	Grade School	Teens	Young Adults	Over 30	Senior Citizens
★★★★★	★★★★★	★★★★★	★★★★★	★★★★★	★★★★★

Duration of Ride: Approximately 7 minutes

Average Wait in Line per 100 People Ahead of You: 5 minutes

Assumes: All simulators operating

Loading Speed: Fast

DESCRIPTION AND COMMENTS   This attraction, now enjoying huge success at Disneyland in California, is so amazing, so real, and so much fun that it just makes you grin and giggle. It is the only Disney ride anywhere for which we have voluntarily waited forty-five minutes in line, not once, but three times in a row. The attraction consists of a ride in a flight simulator modeled after those used to train pilots and astronauts. Guests, supposedly on a little vacation outing in space, are piloted by a droid (android, a.k.a. humanoid, a.k.a. robot) on his first flight with real passengers. Mayhem ensues almost immediately, the scenery flashes by at supersonic speed, and the simulator bucks and pitches. You could swear you were moving at light speed. After several minutes of this, the droid somehow gets the spacecraft landed and you discover you are about ten times happier than you were before you boarded. We would love to see a whole new generation of Disney rides on the order of Star Tours.

TOURING TIPS   If you happen to visit California, it's worth a trip to Disneyland just to experience this ride. If you decide to wait until 1990 at Disney-MGM Studios, you have a lot to look forward to.

Sound Effects Stage

Type of Attraction: Audience participation show, demonstrating sound effects

When to Go: Before noon or after 4 P.M.

Authors' Rating: Funny and informative; ★★★★

Authors' Estimated Appeal by Age Group:

Pre-school	Grade School	Teens	Young Adults	Over 30	Senior Citizens
★★★½	★★★★	★★★★	★★★★	★★★★	★★★★

Duration of Presentation: 20 minutes

Pre-Show Entertainment: Yes; participants are selected from the audience.

Probable Waiting Time: 10–12 minutes

DESCRIPTION AND COMMENTS   A live show where guests are invited on stage for a crash course in becoming sound-effects technicians. The results of their training, always funny, are played back at the end of the show for the audience to enjoy.

TOURING TIPS   The smaller theater makes this show a better early-morning or late-afternoon bet.

Epic Stunt Theater

Type of Attraction: Movie stunt demonstration and action show
When to Go: Between 11 A.M. and 3:30 P.M.
Authors' Rating: Fast-paced and exciting; ★★★★
Authors' Estimated Appeal by Age Group:

Pre-school	Grade School	Teens	Young Adults	Over 30	Senior Citizens
★★★★	★★★★½	★★★★½	★★★★	★★★★	★★★★

Duration of Presentation: 30 minutes
Pre-Show Entertainment: Pending
Probable Waiting Time: None

DESCRIPTION AND COMMENTS   Professional stunt men and women demonstrate some of Hollywood's most exciting and dangerous stunts in an enlightening and riveting production.

TOURING TIPS   Since the Epic Stunt Theater holds 2,000 persons, you can be reasonably sure of getting into any performance you choose, simply by arriving fifteen minutes before show time. Performance times are posted outside the theater as well as being listed on the daily live entertainment handout.

The Studio Tour

Approximately two-thirds of the Disney-MGM Studios is occupied by a working film and television facility, where throughout the year actors, artists, and technicians work on various productions. Everything from TV commercials, specials, and game shows to feature motion pictures are produced here.

Visitors to the Disney-MGM Studios can get a real "behind-the-scenes" education in the methods and technologies of motion picture and television production. The vehicle for this learning experience is a comprehensive tour of the working studios.

At the end of Hollywood Boulevard, next to the Chinese Theater (The Great Movie Ride), guests enter the limited-access area through an ornate studio gate. After viewing a short film introducing them to filmmaking, they board ever-faithful trams for a combination riding and walking tour of the studios.

Wardrobe and Crafts Shops

The Studio tour begins with the wardrobe and crafts shops. Here costumes are designed, created, and stored, as are sets and props. Visitors watch craftsmen from the tram, through special picture windows.

Backlot/Motion Picture Shoot/Catastrophe Canyon

From the shops, the tour proceeds to the winding streets of the backlot, where Western desert canyons and New York City brownstones exist side by side with European villages and modern suburban residential streets. While exploring the backlot, the tour pauses to witness an actual motion-picture shoot.

For many, the highlight of the backlot tour is the passage through Catastrophe Canyon, a special-effects adventure that includes an earthquake, an oil-field fire, a flash flood, and a collapsing bridge.

206

—— *The Walking Tour: Special Effects/ Editing/Audio/Sneak Previews* ——

Having survived Catastrophe Canyon, guests disembark at a rest and refreshment area to catch their breath before finishing the studio tour on foot. First stop is a special effects area, where technicians explain the mechanical and optical tricks that "turn the seemingly impossible into on-screen reality." Included here are rain effects and a miniature naval battle.

A short walk brings guests to the working soundstages, where specially designed and soundproofed observation platforms allow unobtrusive viewing of productions in progress. After explaining the basics of whatever productions are in progress, the guide leads guests through sets from recent hit films.

From the soundstages, the Studio Tour moves to the postproduction area where film editing and audio dubbing take place, and then to a theater where a short film summarizes the entire film production process. The summary film concludes the studio tour. From here, guests can return to Hollywood Boulevard or visit the Animation Building.

Animation Building

The Animation Building is where, for the first time, the public is invited to watch Disney artists at work. Since Disneyland opened in 1955, Walt Disney Productions has been petitioned by its fans to operate an animation studio tour. Finally, after a brief three-and-a-half-decade wait, an admiring public can watch artists create beloved Disney characters. A small gallery and theater assist in explaining the complex process, which includes developing storyboards for story and dialogue planning, and producing the boxcar loads of paintings and drawings needed for animation.

TOURING TIPS   The riding, guided part of the tour takes about an hour, followed by a rest stop and then the walking portion of the tour. The entire tour is guided. We recommend going on the tour first thing in the morning. The tour, incidentally, shuts down about thirty minutes before dark.

—— *Eating at Disney-MGM Studios* ——

Disney-MGM Studios features the Soundstage Restaurant where diners will eat among sets and props, and the Backlot Restaurant with theme dining rooms. Fast food is available from vendors and at eateries along Hollywood Boulevard.

—— *Shopping at Disney-MGM Studios* ——

Shops throughout the park carry movie-oriented merchandise and, of course, Disney trademark souvenir items. Most of the shopping is concentrated on Hollywood Boulevard and consists of movie nostalgia goodies ranging from Jujubes (if you are over 40, you still probably have some stuck in your teeth) to black-and-white postcards of the stars. Unusual shops include a photography studio where guests can be photographed for a mock-up cover of a well-known magazine, a sound studio where guests can make a recording of themselves singing top 40 songs to the accompaniment of a back-up band, and shops selling one-of-a-kind props, costumes, art, and other movie memorabilia. The Animation Gallery, located backstage, markets reproductions of cells from movies and other animation art.

Disney-MGM Studios
One-Day Touring Plan

FOR: **Visitors of all ages**

Until Star Tours opens in 1990, touring Disney-MGM Studios will not be as complicated as touring the Magic Kingdom or EPCOT Center. In addition, all Disney-MGM rides and shows are essentially oriented to the entire family; this can eliminate differences of opinion about how to spend the day. Where in the Magic Kingdom Mom and Dad want to see the Hall of Presidents, big Sis is hot to ride Space Mountain, and the pre-school twins are clamoring for Dumbo the Flying Elephant, at Disney-MGM Studios the whole family can pretty much see and enjoy everything together.

The following Touring Plan assumes a willingness to experience all major rides and shows.

1. Call Walt Disney World information (407) 824-4321 the night before you go for opening and closing times.
2. Arrive 45 minutes before the stated opening time, buy your admission and wait to be admitted to the park.
3. Upon admission stop at the Guest Relations complex to the left of the main entrance and pick up a schedule of live performances and special events.
4. Proceed to the end of Hollywood Boulevard to the gate at the right of the Chinese Theater and wait to be admitted to the Studios Tour. Have all children visit the restrooms before the tour.
5. Take the studio tour.
6. Following the tour, visit the Animation Building.

NOTE: By this time of day during the busier periods of the year, the park will be fairly crowded. Lines for the remaining rides and shows may appear long, but should move quickly due to the large capacities of the various attractions. Since there are numerically fewer attractions at Disney-MGM than at the other parks, the crowds will be more concentrated. If a line seems unusually long, ask a Disney-MGM attendant what the estimated wait is. If the wait is too long try the same attraction again while a show at the Epic Stunt Theater is in progress or while a parade or some special event is going on. All of these activities serve to draw people away from the lines.

7. Try the show at the Sound Effects Stage.
8. Take in a performance at the Disney Television Theater.
9. Ride the Great Movie Ride.
10. See the show at the Epic Stunt Theater. If one is not scheduled for a while, grab a bite or tour Hollywood Boulevard until showtime.
11. Enjoy special events and entertainment as per your daily entertainment schedule.

APPENDIX—
Special Tours and Nightlife

Behind the Scenes Tours at Walt Disney World

Interested adults (16 and over) can book guided walking tours exploring respectively the architecture of the international pavilions of EPCOT Center, and/or Walt Disney World's gardens, horticulture, and landscaping. Each tour lasts 3½ hours and participants must have an EPCOT Center admission ticket. For reservations call (407) 345-5860.

For children 10–15 years old, there are a number of special learning programs available. In addition to being educational, these 6½-hour programs also give Mom and Dad a little time to themselves. Call (407) 345-5860 well in advance for information and reservations.

Walt Disney World at Night

The Disney folks contrive so cleverly to exhaust you during the day that the mere thought of night activity sends most visitors into anaphylactic shock. For the hearty and the nocturnal, however, there is a lot to do in the evenings at Walt Disney World.

In the Parks

At EPCOT Center the major evening event is IllumiNations, a mixed-media laser and fireworks show at the World Showcase Lagoon. Showtime is listed on the daily entertainment and special events schedule.

In the Magic Kingdom there is the ever-popular Main Street Electrical Parade and Fantasy in the Sky Fireworks. Consult the daily entertainment schedule for performance times.

At the Hotels

At waterside at each of the hotels connected by monorail is the Bay Lake and Seven Seas Lagoon Floating Electrical Pageant.

At Pleasure Island

Pleasure Island, Walt Disney World's nighttime entertainment complex, features six nightclubs, including a roller rink and a non-alcoholic club for minors, for one admission price. Dance to rock or country, or take in a showbar performance, or see a movie. Pleasure Island is located in Walt Disney World Village and is accessible from the theme parks and from the Transportation and Ticket Center by shuttle bus.

—— Walt Disney World Dinner Theaters ——

There are several dinner theater shows each night at Walt Disney World. Reservations can be made on the day of the show at any of the resort hotels, or by calling (407) 824-8000 for the *Top of the World* and the *Polynesian Revue* and (407) 824-2748 for the *Hoop Dee Doo Revue*. Visitors with reservations for a Walt Disney World lodging property can make reservations prior to arrival by calling the same numbers. Getting reservations for *Top of the World* and *Polynesian Revue* presentations is not too tough. Getting a reservation to the *Hoop Dee Doo Revue* is a trick of the first order.

Top of the World

Top of The World, situated atop the Contemporary Resort Hotel, features a creative menu with entrees such as roast duck, shrimp brochette and steak combination, seafood catch of the day, prime rib, and veal with sausage. Unlike most other dinner theaters, the pace is unhurried and the menu provides plenty of variety. The food is good and nicely presented, and the service is excellent.

The entertainment consists of dinner music and dancing to a live orchestra (playing primarily easy-listening standards), followed by a lively stage show featuring showtunes from Broadway and limited choreography. The presentation is professional and straightforward, but not particularly imaginative or compelling. *Top of the World* appeals to a more mature audience and we do not recommend the show for children under twelve. Cost is about $40.00 per person plus drinks and tips. Gentlemen are required to wear jackets (but not ties).

The Polynesian Revue

Presented nightly at the Polynesian Village, the evening consists of a "Polynesian style" all-you-can-eat meal followed by south seas island native dancing. The dancing is interesting and largely authentic, and the dancers are comely but definitely PG in the Disney tradition. We think the show has its moments and that the meal is adequate, but that neither are particularly special. Cost per adult is about $30.00. If you really enjoy this type of entertainment, and experience a problem getting a reservation for the Polynesian Revue, Sea World presents a similar dinner and show each evening.

Hoop Dee Doo Revue

This show, presented nightly at Pioneer Hall at Fort Wilderness Campgrounds, is by far the best of the Disney dinner shows. The meal, served family-style, consists of barbecued ribs, fried chicken, corn on the cob, and baked beans, along with chips, bread, salad, and dessert. All of these are most satisfactory, though none are good enough, as we say in the South, to "make you want to slap your momma." Portions are generous and service is excellent.

The show consists of western dancehall song, dance, and humor, much in the mold of the *Diamond Horseshoe Jamboree* in the Magic Kingdom, only longer. The cast is talented, energetic, and lovable, each one a memorable character. Between the food, the show, and the happy, appreciative audience, the *Hoop Dee Doo Revue* is a delightful way to spend an evening. Cost per adult is about $30.00.

Now for the bad news. The *Hoop Dee Doo Revue* is sold out months in advance to guests who hold lodging reservations at Walt Disney World properties. If you plan to stay at one of the Walt Disney World hotels, try making your *Hoop Dee Doo* reservations when you book your room. If you have already booked your lodging call as far in advance as possible. For those with accommodations outside of Walt Disney World:

1. Call (407) 824-2748 thirty days prior to visiting. If that does not work:
2. Call (407) 824-2748 at 9 A.M. each morning while you are at Walt Disney World to make a same-day reservation. There are three performances each night, and for all three combined, only three to twenty-four people, total, will be admitted on same-day reservations. If no reservations are available:
3. Show up at Pioneer Hall (no easy task in itself unless you are staying in the Campgrounds) forty-five minutes before showtime (early and late shows are your best bets) and put your name on the standby list. If someone with reservations fails to show, you may be admitted.

If all of this sounds too much like work, try the show at Fort Liberty, a non-Disney attraction on FL 192. Call (407) 351-5151 for reservations.

—— *Other Area Dinner Theater Options* ——

There are a number of dinner theaters within twenty minutes of Walt Disney World. Of these, *Fort Liberty* is a good substitute for the *Hoop Dee Doo Revue. Medieval Times*, featuring mounted knights in combat, is fun and most assuredly different. And *King Henry's Feast* is a fun variety show on the theme of King Henry's birthday celebration. The food at all three of these dinner theaters is both good and plentiful and all three shows are highly recommended. Cost per adult is around $25–30, but discount coupons are readily available at brochure racks and in local tourism periodicals found in motel lobbys. *Fort Liberty* and *King Henry* reservations can be made by calling (407) 351-5151. Call (407) 239-0214 for *Medieval Times*.

A fourth dinner theater, *Mardi Gras*, stages a better Broadway-style show than does Disney's *Top of the World*. Unfortunately, and in contrast to *Top of the World*, the food is mediocre. In addition, *Mardi Gras* guests are literally packed at their tables. The tariff at *Mardi Gras* is about $25 for adults not counting the bar tab. For information or reservations call (407) 351-5151.

The *Bavarian Bierhaus*, roughly situated behind the Wet and Wild Water Park, serves up German specialties, imported beer and lots of "oom pah pah" live music and dancing. The food is reasonably priced and good, and the mood is always happy and upbeat. The experience in general is much like a dinner seating at the German restaurant in EPCOT Center except that the *Bavarian Bierhaus* is less expensive and you can stay as long as you like. There is no admission charge. For information call (407) 351-0191.

Index

Admission
  cost of, 37–38
  credit cards for, 51
  One-Day Ticket, 38
  World Passports, 38, 39
ADVENTURELAND, 68–70
  Jungle Cruise, 69
  Pirates of the Caribbean, 69–70
  Swiss Family Treehouse, 68
  touring tips, 68–70
  Tropical Serenade (Enchanted Tiki Birds), 70
Alcoholic beverages, 55
American Adventure, The, 160–61
American Gardens Stage, 167
American Journeys, 99
Animation Building, 207
Aspirin, 56
Attendance patterns, 20–26
Arriving early, 43

Backlot/Motion Picture Shoot/ Catastrophe Canyon, 206
Backstage Magic, 143
Banking services, 57, 63, 201
Big Thunder Mountain Railroad, 71–72
Boat access
  to Discovery Island, 13
  to Fort Wilderness Campground, 31
  to Magic Kingdom, 31, 34, 61
Body Wars, 153
Bottlenecks, 44. *See also* Crowds
Bus. *See* Shuttle bus

Campgrounds. *See* Fort Wilderness Campground
Canada, 163–64
Captain EO, 149
Caribbean Beach Resort Hotel, 30

Carousel of Progress, 98
Car trouble, 19, 55
Cash, 57
Catastrophe Canyon, 206
Character appearances, 107–9, 167
Character parades, 61, 107–9, 167
Children, 51–54
  baby-sitting for, 52
  facilities for care of, 19, 52, 64
  learning programs for, 213
  lost, 53, 64, 199
  play area, 92
  scary stuff, 51–54, 71, 79, 83, 100
  strollers for, 52, 61, 63, 194, 201
  touring plans for, 127–30, 191–92, 209–10
Chinese Theater, 199
Cigarettes, 56–57
Cinderella Castle, 61, 88
Cinderella's Golden Carrousel, 84
City Hall, 61
CommuniCore, 140–43
Contemporary Resort Hotel, 7, 29–30
Convention Center, Walt Disney World, 30
Country Bear Jamboree, 73
Cranium Command, 153–54
Credit cards, 51
Crowds
  at closing, 43–44, 116, 182
  daily, 24
  longest lines, 43–44
  at opening, 43, 115, 180–81
  seasonal, 20–21
  time of year for, 20–21, 25
  and traffic patterns, 22–24, 115–16, 180–82
  and weather, 21
Currency exchange, 57–58, 201

Davy Crockett's Explorer Canoes, 74–75
Diamond Horseshoe Jamboree, 72–73
Dinner theaters, 168, 214–17
　Hoop Dee Doo Revue, 215–16
　Polynesian Revue, 215
　reservations, 168, 215–16
　Top of the World, 215
Directions, 34
Discovery Island, 12–13
Disney Animation Studios, 207
Disney characters, 107–9, 89–92, 167
Disney Inn, The, 30
Disneyland, 13–16
DISNEY-MGM STUDIOS, 8, 195–210
　best days, 24–26
　closing time of, 201
　compared to Magic Kingdom and EPCOT, 197–98
　Guest Relations, 199
　live entertainment, 199
　maps, 199
　One-Day Touring Plan, 209–10
　Open Access/Movie Theme Park, 201–5
　　Chinese Theater, 199
　　Disney Television Theater, 202–3
　　Epic Stunt Theater, 205
　　Great Movie Ride, 202
　　Hollywood Boulevard, 199, 201
　　Sound Effects Stage, 204–5
　　Star Tours, 203–4
　　touring tips, 201–5
　overview, 197–200
　parking, 36, 199
　Studio Tour, 206–7
Disney Television Theater, 202–3
Dreamflight, 98–99, 101–2
Dumbo, the Flying Elephant, 86–87

Earth Station, 140
Eating
　alternatives, 110–12, 177
　breakfast, 110, 176
　bring your own meals, 112
　dinner, 111–12, 169–77, 214–17
　in Disney-MGM Studios, 208
　in EPCOT Center, 169–77

fast food, 110, 112, 145, 176
　lunch, 111–12, 169–77
　in Magic Kingdom, 110–12
　resort dining information, 19
　snacks, 110–12
Electronic Forum, 142
El Rio del Tiempo, 156, 157
Enchanted Tiki Birds, 70
Energy Exchange, 142
EPCOT, 7
EPCOT Center, 7–8, 39–40, 133–94
　access to, 136
　best days, 24–26
　Future World in, 136, 139–55
　live entertainment, 167–68
　and the Magic Kingdom, 39, 135
　overview, 133–38
　ride information, 165
　summary, 194
　theater information, 166
　World Key Information, 137–38
　World Showcase in, 136, 156–64
EPCOT Computer Central, 141–42
EPCOT Outreach, 143
Epic Stunt Theater, 205

Fantasy Faire Stage, 107
Fantasy Follies, 108
Fantasy in the Sky, 108
FANTASYLAND, 7, 81–88
　Cinderella's Golden Carrousel, 84
　Dumbo, the Flying Elephant, 86–87
　Fantasy Follies, 108
　It's a Small World, 81
　Mad Tea Party, 87
　Magic Journeys, 83
　Mr. Toad's Wild Ride, 84–85
　Peter Pan's Flight, 82–83
　Skyway to Tomorrowland, 82
　Snow White's Scary Adventures, 85
　touring tips, 81–88
　20,000 Leagues Under the Sea, 85–86
Feminine hygiene products, 57
Film, 58
First aid, 64
Fitness Fairgrounds, 154
Floating Electrical Pageant, 108

Florida
    tourism, 20–24
    traffic patterns, 22–24
    weather, 21
Food. *See* Eating
Foreign currency exchange, 57–58, 201
Foreign language assistance, 54, 137
Fort Wilderness Campground, 31
France, 162–63
FRONTIERLAND, 7, 71–76
    Big Thunder Mountain Railroad,
        71–72
    Country Bear Jamboree, 73
    Davy Crockett's Explorer Canoes,
        74–75
    Diamond Horseshoe Jamboree,
        72–73
    Frontierland Shootin' Gallery, 75
    Tom Sawyer Island and Fort Sam
        Clemens, 73–74
    touring tips, 71–76
    Walt Disney World Railroad, 75–76
Frontierland Shootin' Gallery, 75
FutureCom, 143
FUTURE WORLD, 7, 136, 139–55
    CommuniCore, 140–43
        Backstage Magic, 142–43
        Electronic Forum, 142
        Energy Exchange, 142
        EPCOT Computer Central,
            141–42
        EPCOT Outreach, 143
        FutureCom, 143
        Travelport, 142
    Earth Station, 140
    Horizons, 151–52
    Journey into Imagination, 147–49
        Image Works, 148–49
        Journey into Imagination (ride),
            147–48
        Magic Eye Theater: *Captain EO,*
            149
    Land, The, 145–47
        Harvest Theater: *Symbiosis,*
            146–47
        Kitchen Kabaret, 146
        Listen to the Land, 145
    Living Seas, The, 143–44

Spaceship Earth, 136, 139–40
touring tips, 139–55
Universe of Energy, 154–55
Wonders of Life, 152–54
    Body Wars, 153
    Cranium Command, 153–54
    Fitness Fairgrounds, 154
World of Motion, 150–51
    It's Fun to be Free, 150
    TransCenter, 151
Future World Brass, 167

Germany, 159
Golf course, 19, 30
Golf Resort Hotel. *See* Disney Inn, The
Grand Floridian Beach Resort Hotel, 7,
    30
Grand Prix Raceway, 95–96
Grandma Duck's Petting Farm, 91
Great Main Street Electrical Parade,
    108
Great Movie Ride, 202
Guest Relations, 199

Hall of Presidents, 77–78
Handicapped visitors, 54. *See also*
    Wheelchairs
Harvest Theater: *Symbiosis,* 146–47
Haunted Mansion, 78–79
Hollywood Boulevard, 199, 201
Horizons, 151–52
Hotels. *See* Lodging
Hours of operation
    confirmation of, 26, 43
    Disney-MGM Studios, 43
    EPCOT Center, 43
    Magic Kingdom, 43
    opening times, 26–27, 43
    peak capacity, 115

IllumiNations, 167–68
Image Works, 148–49
Impressions de France, 162–63
Italy, 160
It's a Small World, 81
It's Fun to Be Free, 150

Japan, 161

Journey into Imagination (and ride), 147–49
Jungle Cruise, 69

Kids of the Kingdom, 107
Kitchen Kabaret, 146

Land, The, 145–47
LIBERTY SQUARE, 7, 77–80
 Hall of Presidents, 77–78
 Haunted Mansion, 78–79
 Liberty Square Riverboat, 78
 Mike Fink Keelboats, 79–80
 touring tips, 77–80
Liberty Square Riverboat, 78
Listen to the Land, 145
Live entertainment
 in Disney-MGM Studios, 199
 in EPCOT Center, 167–68
 in the Magic Kingdom, 107–9
Living Seas, The, 143–44
Lockers, 55, 61, 63, 194, 199, 201
Lodging, 29–33
 Caribbean Beach Resort, 30
 Contemporary Resort Hotel, 7, 29–30
 costs for, 29–33
 credit cards for, 51
 discount, 33
 Disney Inn (formerly Golf Resort Hotel), 30
 Fort Wilderness Campground, 31
 Grand Floridian Beach Resort, 7, 30
 importance of proximity, 29, 42
 kitchen facilities in, 31
 outside Walt Disney World, 29, 32–33
 Polynesian Village, 7, 29–30
 reservations for, 19
 Walt Disney World Swan Resort, Dolphin Hotel and Convention Center, 30
 in Walt Disney World Village, 31
 Walt Disney World Village Hotel Plaza, 31–32
 Walt Disney World Village Resort (villas), 31

Lost and found, 19, 55, 61, 63, 194, 201

Mad Tea Party, 87
Magic Eye Theater: *Captain EO,* 149
Magic Journeys, 83
MAGIC KINGDOM, 7, 14–16, 59–131
 Adventureland, 68–70
 best days, 24–26
 Fantasyland, 81–88
 Frontierland, 71–76
 guide to, 61
 Liberty Square, 77–80
 live entertainment, 107–9
 Main Street, U.S.A., 63–67
 Mickey's Birthdayland, 89–92
 ride information, 101–4
 summary, 131
 theater information, 105–6
 Tomorrowland, 93–100
MAIN STREET, U.S.A., 7, 63–67
 City Hall, 61, 63
 closing hours, 26–27
 Main Street Cinema, 65–66
 Main Street Electrical Parade, 108
 Main Street Parade, 108
 Main Street vehicles, 66
 opening hours, 63
 Penny Arcade, 66
 touring tips, 63–67
 Train Station, 61
 Transportation rides, 66
 Walt Disney Story, 65
 Walt Disney World Railroad, 63, 64–65
Map of Walt Disney World area, 35
Messages, 54
Mexico, 156–57
MICKEY'S BIRTHDAYLAND, 7, 89–92
 Mickey's Hollywood Theater, 90–91
 Mickey's Surprise Party, 90–91
 Grandma Duck's Petting Farm, 91
Mike Fink Keelboats, 79–80
Mission to Mars, 100
Mr. Toad's Wild Ride, 84–85
Mixed drinks, 55
Money, 57

Monorail
  to EPCOT Center, 7–8, 34–36, 136
  to Magic Kingdom, 7, 34–36, 61
  unlimited use of, 38
Morocco, 162
Motels. *See* Lodging
Motion picture shoot, 206

Nightlife, 12, 214–17
Norway, 157–58
Not-to-be-missed attractions
  in Disney–MGM Studios, 202–3
  in EPCOT Center, 193
  in Magic Kingdom, 130

O Canada!, 163, 164
OPEN ACCESS/MOVIE THEME PARK,
  201–5
  Chinese Theater, 199
  Disney Television Theater, 202–3
  Epic Stunt Theater, 205
  Great Movie Ride, 202
  Hollywood Boulevard, 201
  Sound effects stage, 204
  Star Tours, 203–4
  touring tips, 201–5

Packed Park Compensation Plan,
  27–28
Parking, 34–36
  at Disney-MGM Studios, 36, 199
  at EPCOT Center, 35–36
  for handicapped visitors, 34, 54
  at Magic Kingdom, 34
  maps, 35
  at River Country, 11
  at Typhoon Lagoon, 36
People's Republic of China, 158–59
Peter Pan's Flight, 82–83
Pets, 58
Pirates of the Caribbean, 69–70
Pleasure Island, 12
Polynesian Revue, 215
Polynesian Village, 7, 29–30
Prescriptions, 56

Rain, 51, 55–56

Reservations, lodging, 19
Reservations, restaurant
  for dinner theaters, 214–16
  at EPCOT Center, 137–38, 140,
    169–71, 184
  at Magic Kingdom, 112
  using WorldKey Information Service,
    137–38, 140, 169–71
Restaurants
  in Adventureland, 70
  credit cards for, 51
  with dinner theaters, 214–17
  in Disney-MGM Studios, 208
  in EPCOT Center, 169–77
  in Fantasyland, 88
  fast-food meals, 110, 112, 145, 176
  in Frontierland, 76
  in Future World, 176–77
  in Liberty Square, 80
  in Main Street, U.S.A., 66–67
  reservations. *See* Reservations
  sit-down meals, 112, 140
  in Theme Resort Hotels, 111
  in Tomorrowland, 100
  in World Showcase, 171–76
Ride information
  in EPCOT Center, 165
  in the Magic Kingdom, 101–4
Rides
  at EPCOT Center, 139, 143, 145,
    147, 150, 151, 153, 154, 157
  at the Magic Kingdom
    capacity, 103
    loading and unloading, 101–3
    popularity, 101
River Country, 10–12

Shopping
  in Disney-MGM Studios, 201, 208
  in EPCOT Center, 178
  in the Magic Kingdom, 62, 113
  in Walt Disney World Village, 31
Shuttle bus
  to Disney-MGM Studios, 199
  to Fort Wilderness Campground, 31
  to River Country, 11
  to Typhoon Lagoon, 9

Shuttle bus (*continued*)
  from Disney Inn, 30
  from hotel, 36
  from Walt Disney World Village, 31
Skyleidoscope, 168
Skyway to Fantasyland, 96
Skyway to Tomorrowland, 82
Snow White's Scary Adventures, 85
Sound effects stage, 204
Space Mountain, 93–95
Spaceship Earth, 136, 139–40
Special events, 61
  and traffic patterns, 116
Special tours. *See* Tours
Spirit of America Singers, 107
StarJets, 96–97
Star Tours, 8, 203–4
Steel drum bands, 107
Strollers, 52, 61, 63, 194, 201
Studio Tour, 206–7
Swimming theme parks, 8–12
Swiss Family Treehouse, 68
Symbiosis, 146–47

Theater, dinner, 214–17
Theater information
  in EPCOT Center, 166
  in the Magic Kingdom, 105–6
Theme Resort Hotels
  Caribbean Beach Resort Hotel, 30
  Contemporary Resort Hotel, 29–30
  Disney Inn, The, 30
  Grand Floridian Beach Resort Hotel,
    30
  Polynesian Village, 29–30
Tickets, 37–38
TOMORROWLAND, 7, 93–100
  Carousel of Progress, 98
  Dreamflight, 98–99
  Grand Prix Raceway, 95–96
  Mission to Mars, 100
  Skyway to Fantasyland, 96
  Space Mountain, 93–95
  StarJets, 96–97
  touring tips, 93–100
  WEDway PeopleMover, 97
  World Premier Circle Vision Theater:
    American Journeys, 99

Tomorrowland Terrace Stage, 108
Tom Sawyer Island and Fort Sam
  Clemens, 73–74
Tours
  Behind the Scenes, 213
  Disney-MGM Studios and Studio
    Tours One-Day Touring Plan,
    209–10
  EPCOT Center One-Day Touring
    Plans, 179–92
    One-Day Plan for Adults, 183–88
    Outline Plan for Adults, 189–90
    Outline Plan for Parents with
      Small Children, 191–92
  guided, 213
  learning programs for children, 213
  Magic Kingdom One-Day Touring
    Plans, 114–30
    One-Day Plan for Adults, 117–22
    Outline Plan for Adults, 123–25
    Outline Plan for Parents with
      Small Children, 127–30
  optimum touring situation, 39–42
  tight schedule, 42–44
  touring plans: how they work,
    44–46, 114–16, 179–82
Traffic patterns (crowds), 20–26,
  43–44
  in EPCOT Center, 180–82
  in Florida, 22–24
  in Magic Kingdom, 115–16
Tram
  in Disney-MGM Studios, 36, 199
  in EPCOT Center, 136
  from hotel, 36
  in Typhoon Lagoon, 36
TransCenter, 151
Travelport, 142
*Tropical Serenade (Enchanted Tiki
  Birds),* 70
20,000 Leagues Under the Sea, 85–86
Typhoon Lagoon, 8–10, 11–12
  best days, 10, 24–26
  parking, 36
  touring tips, 9–10
Typhoon Mountain, 9

United Kingdom, 163

United States, 160–61
Universe of Energy, 154–55
Upalazy River, 9

Visitors with special needs, 19, 54–58
  car trouble, 19, 55
  currency exchange, 57–58, 63, 201
  foreign language assistance, 54, 137
  handicapped, 54, 61, 63, 131, 194
  lost and found, 55, 63, 201
  messages, 54
  wheelchairs, 54, 61, 63, 131, 194,
    201

Walt Disney Story, 65
Walt Disney World, 6–16
  additional information, 19
  compared to Disneyland, 13–16
  hours of operation, 26–27
  map, 35
Walt Disney World Railroad, 7, 63,
  64–65, 75–76
Walt Disney World Village, 31
  access by car or shuttle bus, 31
  lodging, 31
  separate entrance, 34
  shopping in, 31
Walt Disney World Village Hotel Plaza,
  31–32
Walt Disney World Village Resort
  (villas), 31

Wardrobe and craft shops, 206
Water theme parks, 8–12
Weather, 21
WEDway PeopleMover, 97
Wheelchairs, 54, 61, 63, 131, 194, 201
Wonders of China, 159
Wonders of Life, 152–54
WorldKey Information Service,
  137–38, 140
World of Motion, 150–51
WORLD SHOWCASE, 7, 136, 156–64
  access to, 156
  Canada, 163–64
    O Canada!, 164
  France, 162–63
    Impressions de France, 162–63
  Germany, 159
  Italy, 160
  Japan, 161
  Mexico, 156–57
    El Rio Del Tiempo, 156, 157
  Morocco, 162
  Norway, 157–58
    Maelstrom, 157–58
  People's Republic of China, 158–59
    Wonders of China, 159
  touring tips, 156–64
  United Kingdom, 163
  United States, 160–61
    The American Adventure, 160–61
World Showcase Lagoon, 167–68

— *About the Authors* —

Bob Sehlinger is a management consultant and author of five successful books on travel and recreation. John Finley is a twenty-year newspaper veteran, feature writer, and former travel and restaurant critic of the Pulitzer Prize–winning *Courier Journal* of Louisville, Kentucky.